Ripples from Iceland

914.91
L

Ripples

from Iceland

AMALIA LÍNDAL

NEW YORK

W · W · NORTON & COMPANY · INC ·

For Baldur

Contents

Photographs between pages 112–113 **and 144–145**

Preface

EVER SINCE MY ARRIVAL IN ICELAND IN 1949, I HAVE TRIED TO explain to relatives, friends and acquaintances what it's like to live here, and have found it an impossible task. New-comers to Iceland also ask the same questions, but often they are fortified with some previous knowledge of Iceland gleaned from travel and picture books, histories, technical surveys, studies of its literature and poetry, and from the few Icelandic novels translated into English. Valuable as these sources are, there is, nevertheless, an attitude midway between that of the tourist and the native Icelander which has been publicized very little so far, except in newspaper articles, and which should be included in the picture of modern Iceland.

Because the details of daily life here cannot be written down in a book of this sort, I have limited myself to relating some of my first experiences and have then attempted to cover other aspects of life encountered so often that I regard them as typical of Iceland. It must be remembered, however, that these aspects, though treated separately, are but parts of a shifting whole, for life and conditions in Iceland are changing daily. They have changed while I have been writing this book and are still changing—this I say for the benefit of those who insist, for example, that this year some shops *are* beginning to sell peanuts. Also, this book does not attempt to repeat material already available on Iceland, but to supplement it.

To quiet the murmurs of protests from Icelandic or resident readers, I stress emphatically that this book represents only my viewpoint—that of an American woman resident. Wholly different books could be written by people from other countries who now reside in Iceland. Of course, much depends too on the sex of the writer, his interests and attitude. I write from a housewife's point of view; but an artist, professional or skilled worker in any field would see some things in another light because of his close association with those of his own group. Finally, of course, this book is totally different from what a native Icelander would write, not only in content, but in form and style.

This, then, is Iceland as it has seemed to me from 1949 through July, 1961.

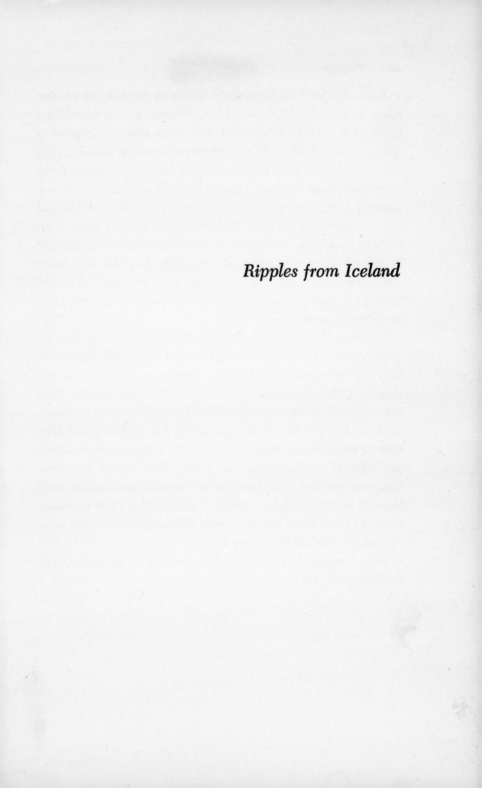

Ripples from Iceland

CHAPTER ONE

How Did I Get Here?

SOME FIFTEEN YEARS AGO, TWO OTHER SOPHOMORES AND I SAT in the smoking room at Boston University and decided we must come to grips with ourselves about final exams. Our nonchalant study habits were making us uneasy. Accordingly, we strolled into town to visit the sort of person who might be expected to know more than a professor—a fortune-teller.

We returned to school with lightened hearts, for Jack declared he had known all along he wouldn't pass, and therefore would no longer worry. Barbara was gratified to learn that she would pass well, and I was pleased to know I would get through by the skin of my teeth, for I hadn't expected that much mercy. The omniscient crone had added that I would marry a tall, fair man and travel to a far country, so my future was all rosy.

Exams descended, and when they departed, little notes began to emanate from the Dean's office: Jack didn't pass; Barbara did, well; and I did, barely.

Next on the agenda for me would be this dreamy guy and a trip to the sunny Mediterranean, unless the lady's second sight had failed her.

Apparently it hadn't, although I find myself still puzzled. Baldur *is* dreamy, especially in the absentminded respect, but the blue Mediterranean doesn't extend to Iceland. I suppose it had never occurred to me that I, who loved warmth and hated fish, would be flown above the blue beside the North Atlantic seaboard to that cold little blot on the map close to Greenland, where Eskimos sit in igloos and fish through the ice.

I was right about the cold, and certainly about the fish being plentiful, but I did not realize that Icelandic customs and ways of living might be as remote in time as its geographical position. When you're twenty-one, "Long Ago and Far Away" means romance, not emigration.

I met my husband-to-be at the International Students' Club in Cambridge, which I attended regularly to participate in the eager, almost passionate discussions with the unaffected foreign students who were so different from the prosaic sophisticates from the Business School of Boston University. At first, I was no more impressed with him than he with me. I found him shy, studious-looking and prone to answer my queries on Iceland in monosyllables, though with careful attention. Our first conversation would have petered out completely had he not gotten a sudden cramp in his leg and groaned.

"Rub it," I advised, "then stand up as quickly as you can before it aches too much." He obeyed, and the cramp went.

We exchanged experiences with leg cramps and went on from there to hobbies and other small things. I found with delight that he loved to hike long distances alone, that he liked to dance, that he did oil paintings, and that he saw a definite relationship between art and engineering. As he talked about his studies and what he hoped to do on his return to Iceland, his eyes began to sparkle and he went on with no prompting, lost in his own enthusiasm.

After this first meeting, I left, in the company of a Chinese student, musing over Baldur's statement that Iceland's artists and writers were as revered as its statesmen. I was studying journalism, but wanted to write novels, as I had told him, and this fact had delighted him. If I was considering further study abroad after college, I should try to visit Iceland, he had said. Decidedly, this prospect deserved further investigation, I thought.

The following Wednesday we met again and he talked uninterruptedly, about the beauties of Iceland, much to the chagrin of my Chinese date who seemed too interested in sampling American womanhood for my comfort. Baldur insisted on walking me to the subway that night.

"I want to build," he said in charmingly accented English, quite fluent now in his enthusiasm. "Iceland is an undeveloped country with great potential. It is an unfinished picture, still unbalanced. It needs industries based on its natural resources to make it more self-sufficient and for export when the fish are scarce. Our main export is fish, you know?"

I didn't know, but I learned. He had not mentioned making money nor becoming a V.I.P. He wanted only to be allowed to give, and to make his country deserve the independence she had won in 1944 after so many years under the dominion of Denmark. And to cap the evening, he asked me out dancing on New Year's Eve, the following weekend.

He was one of the few men I had met who could dance for hours without speaking, lost in the pleasure of moving in rhythm with music. After driving me home in his battered Hudson, he announced, "Some day I'm going to ask you to marry me."

I was dumbfounded and then broke into laughter, while he shrank into himself and looked hurt.

"I'm sorry," I gasped, "but you shouldn't make such statements after such a short acquaintance." American men I had known usually made their honorable intentions known after their passes had proved futile, but Baldur had not even held my hand, except to dance. And after all, I *was* not too unattractive, I told myself.

"I am thirty, and not quite a child," he said. "I know what I want." He *did* kiss me, suddenly, and I went inside the house to ponder on this unique person, so assured in his mission and so direct in his views. I decided he was likely to become a problem in my life, but I would put him through a series of tests guaranteed to winnow him out of my thoughts or fasten him more closely.

Our next date was a six-hour hike, proposed by me. By the fifth hour I was exhausted but determined not to give in first. I would not save his manly pride by confessing myself weaker, neither would he give in. Two minutes before I collapsed, he said, "Let's stop. I can't walk another step." We gazed into the Blue Hills tiredly, and I noted with joy that he felt no shame at being beaten on a hike. We ate something or other at a Howard Johnson's further on and took a late bus back to Boston, still talking. It was the first time I had spent almost twelve uninterrupted hours with a man without becoming bored. On the contrary, I was more exhilarated than ever.

The next step was to match our minds. I had to have a man whose mind I could respect—kisses in the rain notwithstanding. After all, Iceland was a faraway place to live and my parents were apprehensive for their daughter, the only one of three they felt would surely stay close to home.

For ten months we investigated one another's ideas and wrangled over everything, it seems, for in addition to flunking all those glib marriage quizzes, it turned out that he was a lion, astrologically, and I was a bull. The courtship round of the debate showed even results, though, for we agreed on the points that mattered and were prepared to be flexible on the rest. Of course, it struck me as odd that he should remain surprised at several things which I took for granted—that a woman might be interested in values and theories rather than clothes and gossip, that a competitive spirit might exist between women and men, and that Americans are brought up in a tradition of romance which bears little relation to reality. Naturally, these differences between Europeans and Americans were only food for discussion and no more meaningful than that.

As our marriage date drew near, I had spells of feeling trapped. True, we were spending so much time together that our studies were suffering, and it would be much more convenient and pleasant to live together. We had next to no money, for Baldur was at M.I.T. on scholarship and had taken an evening lab job for extra money as well as experience. But how much does a girl give up in marriage, I wondered, when she would perhaps be wiser to work and use her education first before settling in a home?

I saw a pleasant matron with a small child one day in a restaurant and on impulse waylaid her.

"Please help me," I asked. "I am engaged to be married, and I am not sure whether I should marry or finish school and work for a while. You seem so happy with your little boy —I just wanted to ask you whether you have found a compensation in marrying. What shall I do?"

The lady paused and smiled at me very kindly. "You must be sure you love him more than you love yourself," she said. "Otherwise, wait." And she nodded and went to her table.

I asked an older male friend, "Am I supposed to buy a new toothbrush when I marry?" He didn't laugh. He knew that I was asking, "Must I start all anew with nothing of the old which I have always called mine?"

His eyes twinkled, nevertheless. "I don't know. There is no law regarding that; buy one if you want one or need one. You must decide how much you want to change."

My parents, wondered, too, seeing my indecision. They liked Baldur and the naturalness with which he talked to them, but Iceland was so far away. Yet my older sister was finishing medicine at McGill, my younger sister showed promise in commercial art school, and my baby brother had made the high school track team. There would still be a full house even though I went away.

October drew near, and autumn leaves were everywhere. It seemed a good omen to marry in this most beautiful month in New England when nature bursts into her last splendor before winter's cold. The gifts came: household utensils, new clothes, nightgowns instead of pajamas, and I felt very alone. My wedding dress was cream-colored velvet and the house was filled with flowers and candles for the home ceremony. Our rings were carved in diamond facets, long since grown smooth—Baldur's seemed a little loose, and my ring a little tight. I wondered if that was symbolic.

So we were married at my parents' home in Roxbury, promising to love and honor unto our grey hairs (*they* certainly came in a hurry) and betook ourselves off to a hotel in Cambridge. I remember the panicky feeling of registering as Mr. and Mrs., with shiny rings, confetti and new suitcases to prove it. It occurs to me also that we joke about the fear of the bridegroom about to give up his freedom, but hardly give a thought to the bride who may be giving up the only world she has known.

The next morning, Baldur mysteriously disappeared. Unthinkable. Surely not another old pal just in from Iceland! He reappeared with a gleaming gold bracelet for me as a morning gift, an old Icelandic custom. The next day we entered our new home in the Back Bay area of Boston, which was a rented room with kitchen and bath privileges; and I had to tell him about the carrying-over-the-threshold business—an old American custom.

We finished our last semester of school together, but it was another six months before he finished up the lab job he was doing at the same time. I had no trouble finding office jobs to fill up my time and supplement our income, so the time passed quickly. Baldur's thesis was typed by me on schedule —a few days' and nights' work that made us appreciate complete dependence on one another. This feeling of mutual dependence and my ability to land a job both evaporated the moment we reached Iceland, but while they lasted, it was good.

Sometime during that first year in Boston, Baldur invited two young Icelandic students home to dinner. I was very excited and anxious to learn from them what Iceland was really like. They arrived, young, shy, and nice-looking, and ate with us in the kitchen, the landlady having courteously offered to eat earlier that evening. During the meal, except for an occasional bone thrown my way, the conversation was entirely in Icelandic. It didn't much matter whether I was there or not. Afterwards, in our room, it continued along the same lines while I sat and looked sociable. When they left, each youth shook my hand and thanked me for the food. Period.

"Didn't they enjoy themselves?" I asked Baldur afterwards.

"Of course."

"Then why did they thank me only for the food?"

Baldur explained that this was quite proper procedure in Iceland, and so I assumed that their thanks included the pleasant evening and the delectable pleasure of meeting me and looking at me.

One of these young men subsequently rented the room next to ours and took to popping in at all hours to discuss his homework, as both he and Baldur were in chemical engineering at M.I.T. Though I often yearned to know more about Baldur's work, their conversations were technical and in Icelandic, and obviously much more important to both concerned than our newly-married state, so while I could read or mend clothes, I couldn't lounge in pajamas or go to bed. He was very friendly though, and as I got to know him better, I discovered he was one of those who have an unbridled curiosity about everything. I must say I've met few such people since coming to Iceland.

It was he, incidentally, who provided me with my first smell of Iceland. His mother had sent her homesick boy a leg of smoked lamb—the traditional Christmas meat. Moreover, she sent it through the postoffice, whence shortly there-

after appeared a notice that in the future no reeking packages could be mailed to Icelanders without effectively sealed
wrappings.

Our friend easily persuaded the landlady to allow him to
cook his meat in the kitchen. She regretted it when the joint
was boiled, for a greasy smoke crept through the house, and
the odor made one tenant violently nauseous. Since all
attempts to air the house were futile, a fearful atmosphere
surrounded everyone but the two Icelanders who ate the
meat with gusto to the last evil-smelling shred. I tasted it politely, and privately (we were very newly married) thanked
heaven we would eat turkey with my parents the next day.
Now, the turkey is a dream, and the smoked lamb a reality
in our house at Christmas.

*   *   *

Spending the first year of marriage in one room seems to
be an agonizing test of compatibility. How we did it, I can't
imagine, but the days fled by all too fast, and suddenly we
were ready to leave for Iceland.

As my parents bade us tearful goodbyes—a slight mis-
statement, for they had already sweltered in a New York
hotel for two days, and had sat for six more hours in the
waiting room for the takeoff, and so had reached the "Why
don't you go, dammit, so we can miss you" stage—I rather
felt as though the bottom were dropping out of things.

The feeling increased twenty-one hours later when the
plane actually did take off. By then, of course, my parents
had long since given up and returned to Boston, not to know
until later that we'd had a second honeymoon in a luxurious
Long Island hotel.

Unlike most people, I feel that certain situations call for

worry, and though others concerned see no future nor cause for worry, I feel, nevertheless, it is my duty to be properly upset as befits the occasion.

When the plane took off, I immediately felt queasy. As the ground dropped from under us and we skimmed upward into a marshmallow fog, my stomach definitely began a tango. All the other passengers were peering through the windows commenting on the scenery, but I sank back with a certain smug feeling of inevitability. I *knew* I was going to be sick; people *always* are on their first trip. The important thing is to prepare for it. I turned to Baldur.

"Dear, I think I'm going to be sick," I said.

"No, you're not," he said.

"I'm sure I'm going to be sick, I have all the symptoms," I insisted somewhat irritably.

"I've never known you to be sick to your stomach unless you've been eating too much," he amended tenderly.

I summoned a stewardess.

"I think I'm going to be sick," I said.

"Oh, you won't be," she smiled.

"But what if I am?"

"People very rarely get sick on planes, they only think they're going to." She continued down the aisle.

There was a sudden sidewise swoop as we hit an air pocket. I grabbed the hostess on her return trip.

"But what shall I do if I get sick?"

She glanced first at Baldur with some amusement, and then at me.

"Just call me." It was all a huge joke only it wasn't funny.

But it worked. Having shifted the responsibility for my probable condition into the proper hands, I ceased to feel queasy, and cast around for something else to upset me.

After all, I had to give due respect to this momentous trip.

The roaring of the airplane motor suddenly smote my ears. I tried to remember whether the motor had been running when we first got into the air. It undoubtedly had, but I hadn't heard it. I wondered how big the motor was. It sounded as though we were sitting on it, or as though there were no one else in the plane except the motor, but of course *we* were there, Baldur and I, as well as thirty other passengers, two pilots, I hoped, one pretty stewardess, and the one who was so sure I wouldn't be sick.

The plane skidded through an air pocket, and my ears went dead. I hunted frantically for chewing gum, found it, worked my jaws, and with two loud cracks my ears opened again. This kept happening, and though I like gum, there's a limit to everything.

I had my hands quite full. There was the ever-present possibility of being airsick; the thundering noise of the motor, by which I refused to be submerged and against which I kept up a continuous mental resistance; the necessity for chewing frantically every twenty seconds to clear my ears; and last of all, the sudden thought that perhaps the repairing of the plane, which had accounted for the delayed departure, had been incomplete. Daddy had always groused about car tinkerers who have several pieces left over each time they fix something. What if a nut should drop into the Atlantic. Where would I be? Would I have time for those bitter "last thoughts" people are supposed to have? But then I would have blacked out long before I could think them, much less write them. Meanwhile there was still the sickness, the ears, and the motor to be vigilant about. Somewhat wearily I took up the guns again.

"Would you like a cocktail?"

It was the stewardess, the helpful one.

"It will do you good."

I eyed her balefully and accepted.

"You don't feel sick, do you?"

I shook my head in something like defeat.

"Just relax. Enjoy the trip," she said as she passed. I drank the cocktail and fell into a bottomless sleep within five minutes.

When Baldur awakened me for supper, I was numb from sitting. The food must have been eaten by me, for I recall seeing first a full tray and then an empty one, but I don't recommend airborne cocktails for people who want to remember things.

Afterwards, Baldur and the other passengers dropped off to sleep. Even the hostesses kicked off their shoes and curled up. With everyone in the plane sleeping—possibly even the pilots if those things about radar are true—someone must be on guard in case the motor failed. I sat up straight and concentrated on being calm and alert.

By morning, the others were still sleeping, and I was still on guard, though grainy-eyed with fatigue. The virtues of experience and sleeping pills were revealed to me years later.

Despite my vigilance, I did get in a few hours of well-deserved sleep, though I am sure I helped the plane land safely at Reykjavik airport. After fifteen hours aloft, I didn't much care whether we had landed at East Moustache.

CHAPTER TWO

What It Was Like

THE FIRST, THE VERY FIRST THING YOU NOTICE IS THE WIND.
We stumbled out on the landing on July 14, 1949, and the
wind hit us, blowing a penetrating, clear cold that shocked us
fully awake, a hostile, arrogant breeze so clean and sharp it
made the nose twitch. The sun dazzled with its brilliance,
and someone nudged me to get moving. I groped down the
steps, encumbered with coats, umbrella and personal luggage, and alighted on foreign soil—crushed lava better expresses it.

That first long look around made me shrink. There was too
much sky. It stretched overhead and beyond and around,
rimmed in the distance by mountains, a vast, naked landscape in which we seemed to loom as giants. Then I realized

it was the absence of trees that made us seem so dispropor-
tionate. There was plenty of land, though—flat, grey plains
and patches of green velvet dotted with doll houses. Over
all was an unearthly silence and stillness—no trains, little
plane traffic, few cars, no factory smoke to curl in the air.
Only seagulls and the wind.

We filed into a little, whitewashed building where many
papers had to be signed and inspected. It seemed that everyone on the plane who had spoken English now switched to
Icelandic, so I had my first taste of being foreign. I stayed
close to Baldur in the haphazard queue. Finally our docu-
ments were inspected and passed, and we moved to the next
counter.

Luggage was inspected by a silent officer. Such things as
dog-eared slippers and lingerie were exposed briefly to the
public, bottles of spirits were confiscated with courteous explanations—one hopeful soul had brought back a dozen, but
unfortunately they clanked at the wrong moment. The inspected bags, gaping open, dripping with stockings and other
carefully wrapped possessions, were shoved in our direction
for *us* to close—the customs men having done their duty.

There is seldom a thorough scrutiny of luggage, but I know
what lawyers mean when they say the innocent often look
guilty. Once, on a trip to Canada, a customs officer spent a
midnight hour alone with me in the smoking car telling me
of the methods used by smugglers and their detectors. I felt
sure he expected me to surrender the Crown Jewels from
my bag, and never suspected he might have just been trying
to pass the time. Once an Icelandic customs officer did un-
earth a suspicious-looking tube from a lady's bag and de-
manded to know what it was. The lady blushed violently,
but her poker-faced Icelandic husband replied that it was

toothpaste, whereupon the officer appeared satisfied.

Apparently, we carried nothing suspicious, and so eventually we emerged into the waitingroom where Baldur was embraced by a pale young lady with blue eyes and no makeup, his sister Margrét, and by a slightly less pale and handsome young man, her husband Kristinn. A slight commotion below hip level introduced their children, Dóra and Jakob, a little doll of a girl with flaxen hair in a Dutch clip and big blue eyes, and a seven-year-old boy with a rosebud mouth and a huge stare.

We shook hands all around, for such is the custom in Iceland on every occasion, and piled into a taxi. The little girl sat on Baldur's lap and waggled her feet; the little boy just stared. The rapid, somewhat guttural sound of Icelandic filled the air. In self-defense I gazed out of the window at Iceland—grey rocks, a dusty road, not a sign of civilization as the car bumped along toward the town proper. Oh well, the sun was shining—that at least was familiar.

We arrived at a cluster of low, white, concrete boxes, in the hot-springs section of Reykjavik, and entered one of them. During the years I have marveled at the gracefulness that can be achieved in concrete architecture, but at that time when earthquake-proof homes had only recently been required by law inside Reykjavik, little imagination was used in either interior or exterior planning, with rarely any paint but white or grey used on the outsides.

A slender, very erect, old lady with long braids came to meet us, and more of that rattling language with swallowed endings. (In speaking Icelandic, the voice is dropped at the end for a question, and raised questioningly for a statement, and all words are accented on the first syllable.) More handshaking and introductions, and then we were led to the table for dinner.

Over the table I realized why everyone seemed so pale to me. We had left America in July when the temperature had been high in the 90's for days; consequently, my eyes had grown used to sun-tanned people. The Icelanders as a group are among the fairest in the world, being still almost 98 per cent Nordic and some Celtic stock. Also a hot sun seldom endures more than a few days at a time and, even with sun, only in a good summer does the temperature climb into the 70's. Because of climate and custom, Icelanders are not used to outdoor living, nor is there much leisure for sunbathing. Hardly anyone will sit or lie in the sun even if he has the leisure, without some sort of handwork.

Of the immediate family group, only the little Dóra had yellow hair; that of the rest ranged from light to medium brown. There are few real brunettes in Iceland and fewer dark eyes, most eyes being blue, grey, or tawny. I was definitely brunette, so we all did a lot of staring.

The old woman with the braids (people do get old in Iceland, but the term does not imply uselessness or disparagement) was the mother of Baldur's brother-in-law. Her costume, consisting of a stately, full-skirted black dress with a large, flat, silken bow at the bosom, was a national costume, worn with great elegance on festive occasions, and our homecoming was an occasion.

Knowing my sister-in-law, I'm sure that the house had been thoroughly cleaned, waxed and dusted for our arrival. At the time, however, all I noticed was the bareness of painted walls instead of wallpaper, the many, many colors of rugs, upholstery, pillows, plants and paintings—all thrown into over-bright focus by the flood of sun through spotless windows.

I noticed that the food was good, but I was too tired and excited to eat much. Aside from the table conversation, I was still aware of silence—such a complete absence of sound that my ears thrummed with it. Three-year-old Dóra ate her soup unaided, even with an enormous soupspoon the size of a serving spoon. Jakob was still so busy staring he couldn't eat. After a few tentative smiles on my part and one deliberate wink, he grinned and attacked his dinner. At seven years of age even he could manage knife and fork in true European fashion. The American way of eating with just a fork is permitted only to small children, I was informed later. I think it is skillful of children and Americans to manage with only a fork, especially since I can't train myself to eat European style without getting a lapful of potatoes.

Margrét and Kristinn spoke some hesitant English with me, which helped to make me feel at home, and Baldur flung an occasional word in my direction and translated my replies for everyone's benefit. (Many Icelanders have an excellent reading knowledge of English, but little experience in speaking or writing it.) Baldur was naturally bombarded with questions, and I ate and listened uncomprehendingly and relaxed from the trip gratefully.

After dinner, we were shown upstairs to the tiny apartment which my new relatives had given us. The housing shortage here was and still is more acute than in the States, though I didn't realize that till later. Reykjavik has gained more than twenty thousand inhabitants in the last ten years, so it is not surprising that apartments are at a premium.

Our little haven, completed for our arrival, was a dream compared to our room in Boston. It was high with eaved windows that overlooked the ocean and mountains, and was close to the birds who perched on the roof. Six glossy white doors, all closed, led from the entrance room, all with brass car–door handles instead of the familiar doorknobs. (Inside doors in Icelandic homes are often closed. Americans close a door to indicate occupancy or a wish for privacy, whereas Icelanders close all rooms not in immediate use and lock them for privacy. Even though new houses are less drafty, the custom of closed doors still persists.) One door led to the bathroom, which had no bath, another to our sleeping room, another to the livingroom, another to the kitchen, which measured two by three and a half feet of floor space under a sloping roof. (These step-saving kitchens are not recommended for wives who want their husbands to dry dishes, but excellent for husbands who prefer to sit in the outer room with a cup of coffee and watch.) Another door led to a storeroom, where I discovered among other things four lovely silver fox hides which later became a stole for me. After a long time, the grandmother invited me into the sixth room, which was hers, and which satisfied my curiosity in all respects. I watched her put a wooden spinning wheel to good use as she spun undyed wool into huge balls, later to be knitted into socks and mittens for her grandchildren.

Our rooms were bare save for a card table, a wicker chair and the under part of a studio couch, called a "sleeping couch." Because no blankets are used here, there is no place to tuck anything in on most beds. Instead a huge eiderdown-filled bag, sometimes stitched into sections, and always covered with a clean sheeting bag, provides the covering. Judicious kicking distributes the down evenly, thus providing a year-round blanket. Everyone owns his *saeng* as everyone owns his purse. He packs it along for a summer visit to the country, and takes it with him when he marries. It is a cherished and costly personal possession preferred by Icelanders to blankets, though foreigners often find it too hot to sleep under, and complain that it reaches only to the ankles or that the down somehow collects at one end during the night, leaving one's other side quite shivery.

I mentally clothed our crib-width bed in clean sheets and warm blankets and sighed heavily. But no rest for the weary —Baldur wanted out. He had waited four years for this, four years studying in that dirty noisy metropolis, Boston, so he could return to his beloved Iceland. Besides it was only midday.

We went out, and it was lovely. The sun gave an almost white light through the clear air, bleaching some of the color from the grass, turning the road to yellow dust, throwing the white houses into sharp relief against the infinity of blue sky. If you have ever doubted that the earth is round, come to Iceland, and you can see that the sky curves like a cup over the land. It produces a strange, wild effect of freedom. I began to see what Baldur meant.

The human mind can encompass only so much at a given time, however, before it folds up. Mine collapsed twenty minutes later when, freezing with cold—the temperature must have been in the 50's with north winds—I begged Baldur to translate "Let's go home" into Icelandic. He did, and some minutes later we fell into bed. Bed never felt so good, even though it meant a total of less than three feet for two people.

What I remember most about those first days was the capriciousness of the weather. They say in Boston, "If you don't like the weather, wait a minute," but in Iceland it changes before you even decide whether you like it. The sun shone continuously while the wind blew warm, cool, and cold in turns, and in between these changes the rain fell for five minutes, stormed for ten, then ceased abruptly, leaving a sparkle of diamonds on the windows. There is little thunder or lightning in Iceland, and then only during a stormy winter night.

With all these variations, the sun shone day and night. It seems weird to go to bed at midnight with both sun and moon in the sky, and to have no shades at the windows. Shades are still a rarity, curtains or drapes being used for economy's sake, or venetian blinds for those who can afford them. During June and early July, the sun shines all night. As August approaches, however, there is a noticeable twilight period from 11:00 P.M. to 2:00 A.M. Darkness does not mean bedtime in Iceland's summer.

Funny how much a climate can condition you. This was just one of the adjustments I had to make (if draping a woolen blanket before the window can be called an "adjustment") and, fortunately, it was the easiest.

CHAPTER THREE

Thy People, My People

OF THE THIRTY-ODD AMERICAN AND CANADIAN WIVES WHO HAVE come here to settle during the last twenty years, those who found Iceland most familiar were those of Scandinavian parentage or those brought up in Scandinavian communities. These girls comprise only a fourth of the group now. My background did not help me particularly, for while my parents were predominantly of Spanish and French origin, we were brought up in a typical New England community environment.

Some of the American and Canadian wives have come for a specified trial term, and have usually left at the end of that time, convinced that a better living could be made in the States. Others have come to see how they would like Iceland as a home, and have stayed, or divorced and left. It seems a fact that those who have come as complete strangers to Scandinavian life to "take a look" are not bothered by half the frustrations of those who know they are going to stay forever. Baldur and I came here because that was where he was going to spend his life. His urge to go abroad to study and his studies themselves, were all directed solely toward living in Iceland. It goes without saying that we foreign wives married our husbands for themselves, not for a free trip abroad, though undoubtedly their foreignness invested them with a certain glamour.

From letters written to my parents at the time, I can recapture most of the impressions made on me by my first trip to Baldur's home to meet his parents. The girl of those letters seems as strange to me now as the farm and Baldur's family seemed to me then. I feel ashamed and more than a little sad at realizing how coldly I appraised then, and how little I understood; yet these impressions were real ones, when I was a foreigner to Icelandic life.

After a week or so in our new apartment in Reykjavik, we went north toward Akureyri where Baldur had some business to settle. The high point of the trip, however, would be a stopover at his father's farm halfway to Akureyri to show off the new wife he had acquired along with his foreign education.

I never think of that bumpy seven-hour bus ride without remembering two things. One was being vaguely frightened as we tumbled over narrow mountain roads on the fringe of deep precipices and over equally narrow and frail-looking bridges. The Icelandic rural buses are topheavy with wheels set close together so they can travel roads originally built for horse traffic. When crossing a bridge, the sides of the bus hang over the railings; and as I looked down at the ravine and water far below, I had the fearful expectation of falling through space. The other memory is of carsick children and their paper bags flying in the wind.

But there were breathtaking scenes everywhere: green valleys, winding rivers, water falling in crystal streams down the face of a cliff from a cleft high above, whole fields of lava rock, its drabness enlivened by lichens and mosses. There were steep, shaggy mountains seen at close range, scores of silly-looking sheep that stood in the road so that the bus had to stop and honk before they skittered away. There were storybook cows grazing, or sitting in conversational groups, and many of the plump, little horses with their hair cut in bangs over the eyes.

In every valley large enough for grass cultivation nestled a farmhouse, some of modern box-shape, but most built in the traditional three-roofed style—two sections for family quarters and the third for storage—and, close by, wooden, turf-topped huts for cows, horses and sheep. We saw sturdy men and women making hay in every field, the men in dark clothes and the women wearing kerchiefs and housedresses. Summer is the busiest time on the farms as well as the most popular visiting season, so the workers seldom glanced up from their deft and seemingly effortless movements.

Of course the sun and rain continued to play tag across the summer sky. Every few hours we stopped at an inn for food or coffee and, as we resumed the trip, the children would rid themselves of their food.

In contrast to the beauty of the countryside, Reykjavik seems very barren. It is not a pretty place, and we have Ingolfur Arnason to blame for that. This first settler, outlawed from his native Norway as the result of a feud, sailed to Iceland in 874. As he cast overboard the pillars of his highseat from home, he vowed to settle wherever the pillars should land, and so he founded the capital city where it now stands. Some 90,000 people, or half the population of Iceland, are now concentrated in this southwesterly spot where so much of the scenic beauty depends on the skies. On an overcast day and even on a quite cloudless day, there is little to relieve the grimness of the mountains which rim the city. The houses, even the modern "skyscrapers" of eight or ten stories, seem temporary and insignificant against the mountains. One often has the feeling that these evidences of civilization are as important as the buzzing of flies, and that in a few centuries they will disappear as only an episode in the lives of the mountains. On a sun-and-cloud day, however, there is a panorama of shifting hues on mountains and water, shadows and light move perceptibly across the land surface, grass and bushes are alive with motion, and a sunset can be indescribably beautiful.

But it is in the country, and especially around Akureyri, that I am always aware of a serene poetry, a vibrancy of color and form and motion in the scenery, which is quite absent in Reykjavik. It must be this which makes the country dwellers so much more passionately attached to Iceland than the city ones.

We were quiet as the bus entered Baldur's home valley. It looked very much like other valleys we had passed, but I was happy for him and a little nervous in anticipation of the great meeting. These were going to be my close parents from now on, people influential in Baldur's life, whom I prayed I would like and who would like me.

This was the time when I would have been helped by a brief explanation from Baldur about his renowned home farm, the fair name its people held throughout the land, and about the many, many Icelandic travelers who stopped there on their way north to hear the valley news, for his farm was also the mail and telephone center for the district. He might have mentioned the foreign visitors, some scientists, many sportsmen, who came and stayed and remembered the welcome they received long enough to record it in later travel books. Naturally, Baldur did none of those things. He was too busy anticipating seeing the farm and his family again, and, besides, he knew what it was like: it was home, and he had been away a long time.

So all unprepared, I checked my attire. My honeymoon tweed suit had survived the trip unwrinkled, there were no runs in my nylons, polish still gleamed on my loafers, though I wished I could have worn high heels on this first visit. My nail lacquer was unchipped, my lipstick on straight, and the light perfume I had thought suitable for daytime wear still exuded a faint spice. Baldur looked eager and handsome in neat slacks and a suede jacket. He didn't look as though marriage had disagreed with him.

We waited amidst suitcases and portable typewriter on the road as the bus disappeared in a whirl of dust.

I met Baldur's father—a farmer with dreams, who was trained in agriculture and went to work on a sheep ranch ("ranch" is a better word than "farm," for on most of the farms in northern Iceland sheep and horses are raised rather than crops). A growing interest in geology had led Baldur's father to educate himself in his spare time, so that when I met him, he was not only a farmer, but also a renowned geologist in Iceland, known to foreign geologists interested in the rock formations of that part of the country. He was also the leading citizen in his district, to whom neighbors came to get an impartial judgment of their arguments. His interest in geology was an excellent example of the scientific attitude in Iceland which culminated in his day and which now is regarded as obsolete in most respects. I knew nothing of his status or dreams, or that his halting English belied his real understanding of my language. I saw a stocky, elderly man in heavy pants and thick sweater kissing his returned son in unsissified European manner. To me he seemed a replica of Heidi's grandfather with his twinkling blue eyes, white, whiskbroom moustache, and warm, shy smile—an old farmer, I thought.

Then I met Baldur's mother—a vivid, gifted woman, popular and respected, the driving organizer of a number of women's groups in the valley, and the author of a book on housekeeping. Both she and her husband were educated teachers as well. Cold and fatigue had made her an invalid, but despite this she ran the farmhouse and its people—a full-time job and an impossible one during the war when the hired help moved to the cities, leaving no tractor to replace the men, and only one woman to help in the fourteen-room house. She had dreams and hopes very like mine, but without a tenth of my advantages. I knew nothing of this. I saw a gaunt woman in white wrapper and thick cotton stockings, whose rapid conversation was only interrupted by coughing spasms from blue lips. She was kind and seemed anxious to help me feel at home, despite the language barrier. She was eager in her attempts to know me, to ease her mind that I would be good for her son. I did not dream she was so ill, or that she would die a scant year later—still unsatisfied perhaps—or that she might have welcomed a daughter-in-law who, like her, wanted to write and fulfill herself. I saw a bent and unkempt woman who didn't cover her mouth when she coughed.

I entered the large, concrete house, a comfortable improvement over the older house with its turf roof and wooden walls, where Baldur had lived for his first twelve years. That old house, built by his grandfather had small windows, little space, and was heated by peat burned in the kitchen stove. Cold temperatures such as I have never known persisted most of the year but children and adults alike took their chillblains for granted. The newer, tighter, concrete house had larger windows, more rooms, an indoor bathroom, and radiator heating connected with the kitchen stove—a real achievement. The floors were lacquered, and it was adequately furnished for the total of twenty people who lived there, including the family of six. Everywhere there were examples of skilled feminine handwork—woven rugs, embroidered pillows, tablecloths, doilies, and monogrammed bedding.

When I arrived for that first visit, the heat had been turned off for the summer, the bathroom plumbing was faulty, and there was no hot water or soap. There never had been any electricity. I noticed especially the dark Victorian furnishings, past their prime, the dimness and drabness, and a penetrating cold which I felt through my tweed suit. There were congregations of flies in every room, and a mixed odor in the air of fertilizer, clarified lamb fat, and sheep's wool. To me this was hopeless poverty—not that the thought of this comparative poverty made me sympathetic, not at all. If this was all people could achieve in a lifetime and consider themselves prosperous, I thought, then where did I fit in— a "rich," young foreigner beginning married life with a man without a job, brought up with these standards?

It is typical of Icelanders to let a newcomer form his own impressions. They do not build up or degrade a person, or even give an inkling of the sort he is before the meeting. It is up to the newcomer to form his own opinion. That is why people are introduced only by name, with no occupation or reputation added. In this case Baldur's introduction was simply, "These are my parents. This is my home." And hastily I formed my opinions.

As it was well past noontime when we arrived and dinner had been kept waiting for us, we sat down at the table for dinner: a greasy soup, dried fish that tasted like wood splinters, a gluey rhubarb pudding colored an unappetizing purple, and luckily some good boiled fish and potatoes. Melted lamb fat was served over the fish, and had to be rapidly eaten before it reverted to its original waxy state. There was also plenty of bread—white, brown and black—and soft butter, but none with any salt.

It is interesting to note that salt is seldom mentioned in the old days of Iceland. It was never used for legal tender, and people never "broke salt" with one another because salt was relatively unknown, being imported only in small quantities. Meat was salted, if possible, to keep for the winter and so was fish, but the latter was more often wind-dried, and the meat smoked, even the heads of sheep and horses. Butter, bread, cakes, and most food dishes were and still are almost salt-free, and almost everything, including today's hor d'oeuvres and canapés, contain sugar, making the sugar consumption in Iceland among the highest in the world. Such terms as "worth his salt" or "salt of the earth" seemed quite meaningless. If salt meant wealth, then Iceland was truly poor, and yet the people managed somehow. Even now when we go to her house for dinner, my sister-in-law brings out the saltcellar solely for me—in the salt and pepper shakers I gave her as a gift.

At the table there was much slurping of soup and reaching for the serving dishes. The soup spoons were impossible to maneuver. If you sipped from the side, the soup poured over your chin, and if you put the whole spoon in your mouth, the corners of your mouth hurt for hours. There were no napkins but the backs of hands. I used my spice-scented handkerchief as unobtrusively as possible.

Warmed by the dinner and determined to ignore the still pungent air, I settled down with a book while Baldur went off to see the farm and talk with his parents. The well-fed flies buzzed around me and banged into the window. The window was sealed shut, and though I attacked the flies viciously with a newspaper, there was nowhere for them to go but back to the window glass. Soon I was rigid with rage and a hopelessness that barely covered tears. I was going home. I wouldn't stay. But I was a thousand miles from home and here to stay for life, or lose Baldur.

After a while, the effect of having consumed so many liquids made itself felt, and I proceeded to the bathroom. It was freezing there, and bare except for the usual conveniences, the most imperative one being by the window. The window itself was low, so you could get a good view, and the curtains resembled fish netting. But after all, Icelanders are not squeamish about bathrooms and things.

Several people were taking in hay a few yards away. An old raggedy man with a rake passed close to the window, glanced in casually, and proceeded on his way. Next came a little girl and a woman, who also looked in. As I say, I had a good view. I wondered whether I should wave a gay handkerchief at the passersby. After another few minutes, during which no one passed by, I escaped from the bathroom and returned to the room allotted us for sleeping.

Baldur returned along with the children who, when they saw our suitcases, began to jump on and off with shrieks of enjoyment. Great fun. I was ready to cry. They were beautifully matched pieces of luggage given us as wedding gifts and hardly used. Everyone seemed pleased that the children were enjoying themselves. Even Baldur said nothing. I had already been unappreciative enough without adding complaints about this, so I was silent, watching their shoes scrape and scratch the polished surfaces.

At this point coffee hour came, and the suitcases were spared. I was famished, for I had eaten little of the noon meal. A huge, jam-filled layer cake with whipped cream frosting was served. I accepted gratefully, all good temper restored, dove in hungrily, then froze. The cream was sour and of the consistency of butter. Resolutely I began to breathe through my mouth and finished every crumb on the plate.

Meanwhile, conversation ebbed and flowed, engrossing everyone's attention but mine. It was all Icelandic to me. I smiled and smiled until my face ached.

By nightfall I had completed a staggering list of gripes and was determined to go home that very evening with or without a divorce. I was hysterical about it, if you can be hysterical in whispers. Baldur was caught in the middle, but nevertheless persuaded me to stay at least until the next day. And that did it. By the next day I began to accept things for what they were, and felt much better.

This change in attitude was not miraculous. It was simply that, having once broken bread with strangers and having slept in their house, one's feeling of distance diminishes and his perspective thaws. A number of sober and enlightening insights followed, so that never in subsequent visits did I have that initial sensation of isolation.

First of all, Ruth's reply to Naomi: "Whither thou goest, I will go" was not to be taken literally. This was Baldur's parents' home, not ours, and we could live any way we chose. Good manners as I knew them were merely the veneer of civilized life and would be barriers to me until I learned to place less value on them. I was expected to conform somewhat, but I didn't have to go overboard.

After that first trip north, which included a month's stay in Akureyri, I began to see that all the people I met were honest and hardworking, sincere and kind, and free from evil intent and doing. Their worries were severe illness, the failure of the hay crop and a poor herring season. Against these, my little tribulations were not important at all—except to me. For instance, no one resented my having half a dozen pairs of shoes to their one carefully tended pair, because everyone knows that Americans are rich. Yet my "riches" often embarrassed me, and I wanted to give everything to those who had less, assuming that they wanted them too. Then the nasty consideration arose: These things mean more to me because I have always had them, so I'll keep them as long as they last, knowing they will not be replaced. I cannot give to everyone, for then I will have nothing. They are more used to living with conditions here than I am, and I will learn soon enough. Why hasten the process?

I decided to serve only two meals a day instead of Iceland's five; to go on wearing lipstick so long as my supply lasted (and be a "painted" woman among the pale faces); to keep my nails at Manchu length; to wear slacks to the grocery store (though I was informed that only men and camp followers wore "pants"); to wear stockings instead of ankle-sox with high heels; to keep my hair fixed becomingly; to take several baths a week at the risk of being called too clean (that alone must have really run up my in-laws oil bills, but they never mentioned it); to continue smoking, though it wasn't fashionable then for women to smoke, and though cigarettes cost about 60 cents per package; to use napkins at every meal, and to keep a good supply of handkerchiefs since Kleenex did not exist.

Now twelve years later, I take stock again. I find myself a conservatively, if not dowdily dressed housewife with "noble," harsh hands (with short, unpolished nails), preparing five meals a day, wearing lipstick only when going out, wearing skirts to the grocery store (though many Icelandic ladies of good repute now wear slacks or shorts and tell *me* it's the latest fashion). Now they wear more makeup than I and visit their hairdresser, while I wash and set my own hair when I find time. Baths are no problem, but there is no luxurious dawdling about them now. Paper napkins are too expensive, so we have cloth napkins for Sunday, and a community one for daily use, and germs don't bother me a bit. I still smoke, though my throat and pocketbook tell me I shouldn't. At least I keep buying handkerchiefs—probably own more than anyone I know—and take infinite pleasure in washing and ironing and scenting them. On most trips to the States, I look like a "refugee," and marvel that Americans are so well dressed! And I was the one who wasn't going to change!

I think one of the most difficult things for newcomers to Iceland to adjust to is the food. Such items as bacon (thickly sliced, more fat than lean, inadequately cured, often having a fishy taste, because of the pig's diet, and costing five cents a slice), ham, pork, veal, and beef immediately disappeared from our menu when we arrived because of their high prices.

I developed a taste for horsemeat, which is generally much more tender than Icelandic beef, and used to fill the freezer of our refrigerator each fall with a quarter of a horse sent us from the country; the rest we salted in an enamel pail. Once with trepidation we fed horsemeat to Mother, who is finicky about foods. She thought it was corned beef. The fat of the horse we have used for frying and one year for Christmas baking when there was a margarine shortage. My Christmas cookies were edible that year but rather oily. (Crisco is available but costs four to five times the price of margarine.) We ate whalemeat for some years, but because it is often unavailable, as is liver, here in Kopavogur, I've lost the habit of buying it, though it is quite inexpensive. Ground horsemeat usually substitutes for ground beef in my meatball or spaghetti recipes and tastes fine, seasoned with sage (sent by Mother) as a change.

Icelandic lamb is our staple meat: fresh, ground, salted, smoked, or in sausages and frankfurters, and mixed with spice and potato flour in a meat paste which can be fried up into stiff meatballs. But I cannot force myself to eat smoked lambs' heads. The sight of such a head with eyes and eyelashes complete, reposing on a plate, fills me with repulsion, as does a plate of gelatinous fish cheeks, boiled.

I've grown to like all kinds of fish except herring (too many small bones), for Icelandic fish is better than almost any fish I tasted in Boston and, naturally, inexpensive. Skýr, similar to cottage cheese, is a favorite of most Icelanders. High in protein and calcium, it is easy to prepare and can complete any meal, but I don't like it. It tastes to me like ground chalk mixed with facial cream. Rhubarb I hated in the States, but now I cook it as the Icelanders do with po-

tato flour, sugar, and red food coloring, and I like it. I
thought it amusing to see thin, hot egg-nog poured into a
soupbowl and called egg soup, cocoa served similarly and
called cocoa soup; but I like these soups, though I prefer
to drink them cold in a glass. Potatoes are the main starchy
vegetable here, and are generally boiled. If mashed, they are
sweetened. Macaroni is sometimes used, but always in a
sweet white sauce, never with cheese, tomatoes or meat. Rice
is used only as a dessert pudding, but very seldom served
buttered and salted or mixed with tomatoes and seasonings.
Mayonnaise became popular a few years back, but it is
usually mixed with whipped cream rather than spices. Most
Icelandic canapés are sweet rather than salty or sour, and
foreigners usually feel glutted with sugared foods after living here a short time.

A recent United Nations report listed Iceland as having
the highest protein and calorie consumption of western
Europe and the United States. The conclusion was drawn
that therefore Icelanders eat very well. I agree that the protein intake is high, with all the fish, meat, skýr, dried peas,
and eggs used in baking. (Eggs cost eight cents apiece and
are rarely eaten plain, only used in cooking. When we eat
out, I would rather have half a dozen scrambled eggs and
as many slices of bacon than anything else to give me that
luxurious feeling, for such a dish costs just as much as roast
beef.) The carbohydrate consumption is also high, with potatoes, bread and cakes daily, and much use of sago, corn-
starch and potato flour for thickening. Icelanders are well
filled, but not well nourished, unless they take vitamins and
cod-liver oil, or are wealthy enough to afford imported fruits
and expensive fresh or canned vegetables daily.

Repeatedly I have been told that, because Icelandic foods are cheaper, there is no relation between living standards here and in the States, but I maintain that Americans could cut their food bills in half if they ate and cooked as the Icelanders do: made their puddings, cookies, crackers, cakes, and often bread, as well as soups from scratch instead of from packages; eliminated breakfast cereals, except oatmeal, and bacon and eggs and salads from the menu; made all their own mayonnaise; ate one vegetable three times a week; gave fruit to the children once a week (none for adults, of course); and bought ice cream and soft drinks only on holidays. Twelve stewed prunes can serve three American adults for breakfast fruit, but twelve prunes stewed with potato flour, sugar and water provide six soupbowl servings of dessert once a week, for prunes are expensive. Pick a quart of crowberries or blueberries in an afternoon, cook and strain them, cook the juice with potato flour and sugar, and you have an inexpensive and filling sweet soup for the whole family—if you want to take the time.

Icelandic women seldom throw away meat or fish bones unless they have first been used for soup, and many women spend a few days each fall filling the intestines and stomachs of lambs with mixtures of ground meat, lamb fat, blood and meal, to make their winter supply of cold cuts. I am not that clever but, if I do have the time, I try to make rhubarb jam in quantity at the end of the summer to save buying many jars of fruit jam during the year. Some things in Iceland probably are cheaper because of the way they are marketed: cheese is unsliced, bread is unsliced and usually unpackaged, eggs of mixed sizes are available by weight in paper bags, and most soft foods are individually weighed and measured, not packaged at all.

As can be expected, both shopping and cooking take a long time in Iceland, but one gets used to the change.

* * *

I wonder when the importance of well-kept hands was subordinated to preparing satisfying, economical meals; when a lively interest in the world at large became secondary to a woman's place in the home; when the discouraging and sporadic attempts to learn Icelandic became a driving need for communication. Perhaps it began when I stopped asking women I had just met, "And what do *you* do?," exactly as I asked men about their professions. Or perhaps it began the second summer here when I began writing a novel on the north country. An old fellow whom Baldur knew laughed at hearing this, poked Baldur in the ribs and said, "Wait till she has children. *Then* she'll have something to do!"

CHAPTER FOUR

Not Again!

IN ICELAND, CHILDBIRTH IS CONSIDERED SO STRICTLY A WOMAN'S
affair, even to the actual delivery of the child, that, in all the
wide corridors of the state maternity hospital, there is no
sweat box for expectant fathers. In fact, they don't even feel
it necessary to take a day off and worry. No sir. They go
about their business of earning the daily bread and, come
to think of it, they're probably working for that extra mouth
before it arrives. Maybe they're practical and farsighted.

At any rate, in May, 1951, after eight lighthearted months
of being pregnant or "having something to do," as the farmer
said, slight complications impelled me to call the hospital.
Apparently ballet leaps and baby cupboard carpentry are
not the best activities for heavily laden women, so I was

invited to come and stay overnight for observation.

After the supper dishes were done, Baldur ran downstairs to his sister's apartment and telephoned the fire department for their stretcher. This basket-coffin affair is required by the hospital for the arrival of expectant mothers. In case of premature birth, it is preferred as being more sterile than a taxi. When such a basket emerges from a house, all the neighborhood children collect to gape, and curtains at windows are nudged unobtrusively apart. I smiled and waved at the children and felt like a fool.

I was en route to the National Hospital, the largest in Reykjavik, which at that time had the only maternity building. Now a new city maternity hospital has been added and a dozen private maternity homes have been set up in the town, all quite modern and comfortable, so I am told—but still the maternity wards are overcrowded. Because I come from America and because of my doctor sister, I have always felt safer in the big medical center, where all emergencies could be handled on the spot. No home delivery for me, with the fear of a blue baby having to be rushed to the hospital for oxygen.

There was as usual little space at the hospital, so I was ensconced on an examining table in the operating room (used for operations, not for childbirths) to spend the night resting. Around midnight when I was completely bored, a student nurse came in.

"How is your labor coming?" she asked in Icelandic.

"I'm not in labor," I explained.

She shook her head, puzzled no doubt by my Icelandic, and began to physic and shave me for the non-imminent ordeal. I was so mad I couldn't find words to squelch her. Finally she departed triumphantly with her pans, and labor started abruptly. I was as surprised as she wasn't.

I put down my forbidden cigarette—no smoking is allowed except in the lavatory—hunted through my handbag for pencil and paper and began methodically clocking my "contractions," as the books prescribe. After a few hours I got terribly lonely. People kept scurrying past the door, but no one looked in. I didn't really need help, but moral support, so I rang the bell and a nurse came. She listened to my stumbling recital in Icelandic, smiled, nodded and left, never to return. It is maddening not to be able to speak English in a crisis. I became in turns more lonely, more indignant, and more pained. I tried to sit up, but as I touched the wall, the table under me rolled silently to the middle of the room. I sat up anyway and considered stalking into the corridor to demand company, but a sudden spasm reminded me I was in no condition to hop down. Back to paper and pencil again.

At one point in infinity a little student nurse came in who also spoke no English. She was the belated "company." We smiled at each other, and she sat down beside me and read *True Love Stories* in Icelandic with great enjoyment. Here she was at the beginning and I was at the end, so to speak. It didn't make for congeniality, so I let her read undisillusioned. When she finished her story, she got up and left, and I said goodbye.

When I was absolutely sure I'd reached the second stage of labor, I rang for the doctor, who *could* speak English. A nurse came in, said it was much too soon for a first baby, that the doctor had had a hard night and was resting. Then she started to leave.

"Það *er* að koma. Ég *veit* það!" (It *is* coming. I *know* it!), I insisted. She turned with a harried expression, snatched up the modesty sheet, and gasped. "Ekki láttu það koma!"

(Don't let it come!), she said. Christmas!

She summoned two other ladies, and they all put on rubber gloves and stood around looking at me anxiously, hoping the doctor would hurry. I was equally anxious. What if none of them had ever handled a delivery before! I tried to remember: After the baby comes, tie the cord in two places with sterile twine and cut in between the knots—the second knot is so I won't bleed to death before the placenta comes. Wait for the afterbirth, and—a blank. I couldn't remember. It didn't seem fair that I should have to remember! The doctor still hadn't arisen from his couch, and I was about to burst into a thousand pieces in a lonely, lonely world far from home.

Then, like a radiant being, or so he seemed to me, the *doctor* appeared, pale, haggard, but very capable-looking. I reached out and clutched his hand in an ecstasy of relief —and so help me, he blushed scarlet and dropped my hand on the table. "You jerk," I thought, "I'm not making a pass at you!" (Classes in psychology have just recently begun in the university medical school. I was nine years too soon for this doctor.) I did not cry, feeling it undignified to cry in public, but I made no further "passes." Actually, I had wanted to hold the wrong hand, for it is the midwife who delivers the baby, and the doctor who regulates anaesthesia.

Within fifteen minutes it was all over. They put my little mite in an incubator for five minutes. He weighed only three and a half pounds, but the hospital's two regular incubators were already being used by twin "premies." Then they laid him beside me and left us. There is no peace that equals that following a successful birth. My son lay on his back, opened his eyes, turned his head toward the sun streaming in at the window and stretched his arms wide before falling asleep. He was a beautiful baby, pink and yellow and downy as a peach. (The yellowness was due to an iron deficiency.)

Meanwhile, Baldur, sound asleep at home, was awakened by the doctor, calling to tell him the news. I didn't see him till the three o'clock visiting hour, and it was just as well because there was no bed upstairs for me before then. All told, I reclined eighteen hours on that table. It's a wonder I didn't get a backache.

Upstairs I was initiated into the hospital routine that remained unchanged during all of my visits: Up at six to feed the babies; seven o'clock, wash the face and brush teeth and take temperatures (oral thermometers do not exist in Iceland). Eight o'clock means a glass of milk, salted oatmeal with no sugar and two slices of bread and butter. Then the bedpan festival with results expected, and no modesty screens. Ten o'clock brings the babies again, and after that the student nurses return the flowers which have spent the night on the hall radiator. Then the nurses dust and straighten the room and give everyone water to drink. (Still no coffee, mind you, and this is Iceland!) A pair of nurses come to make the beds, tucking the sheets so tightly that you can't wiggle a toe. They depart and another nurse glances in for a last check on neatness. Everything is in tip-top shape now except the guinea pigs. Then a tattoo of rubber-soled feet down the hall, the door swishes open and the doctor marches in, followed by a couple of stony-faced internes and a prescription nurse, who stands meekly by his side.

This was the best time of day, for the kindly, grey-haired head doctor was a familiar face and a good friend. Though he invariably addressed me as Mrs. Líndal (the other doctors don't address anyone by name) in delightful old-fashioned formality, he never failed to listen attentively to any and all brain waves I had, and to give thoughtful and complete answers. Maybe he used psychology on me, but I think he's *wonderful*, though I hope I won't see him anymore for a while. He moves from bed to bed examining charts, asking brief questions, instructing the nurse on diet and drugs. The internes stand like robots, occasionally fidgeting, occasionally having an alert, unprofessional gleam in their eyes.

The patients never complain without good cause, and always apologetically, though they may have tossed and groaned all night. They are wonderful sufferers who accept with a resigned shrug being left, with stiches, on a bedpan for an hour. When the doctor's brigade leaves, we kick off the sheets and wiggle our toes.

Twelve o'clock brings dinner: meat or boiled fish and potatoes, a sweet soup, and milk for the human cows. Still no coffee, and no cigarette either.

Two o'clock is babies. It sounds like a zoo when the nursery doors are opened. Then the sound of rubber casters as braces of two to six cribs are wheeled down the corridor and into the rooms. The babies are so funny. Some feed diffidently; others break into a sweat because they can't get filled fast enough; and others, like my first, lie sweetly and determinedly asleep during the whole feeding. But the nurses took care of that. They flicked him on the soles of his feet and spanked his four-inch bottom until I burst into tears and told them to stop hitting my baby. "It doesn't hurt him. He *has* to eat," they said. He did, for a few seconds at a time. They finally started supplementing his feedings with milk from an eye dropper.

Coffee time comes at 2:30: more bread decorated with a slice of meat or tomato and egg or simply a prune. And *milk*.

At three o'clock the trays are cleared away, and a feeling

of expectation lightens the air. Then the husbands or fiancés appear, or friends if the husband cannot get off from work. The saddest thing in the world is that unwed mother whom no one visits. She turns to the wall with her book during visiting hours. The women from out of town also have no visitors, but they are more companionable than anyone else in the room.

From four o'clock to six, we are left alone. Some order bedpans (I hate to keep mentioning it, but hospital life seems to consist mainly of eating and elimination), and others who have lain in bed for four days get up shakily, pass their hands over the seeming thinness of their bodies and walk to the lavatory. Then back to bed, where one may muse.

The overcrowded hospital has no space for a community room for convalescents and I doubt that any was included in the original plans. There is an armchair in each room and several in the corridor for those no longer bedridden, but there is no reading matter. The patients sit or pace, never speaking unless they are from the same room. The ladies' aid in the hospital might well subscribe to magazines for patients' use. And convalescents should be allowed to roll bandages or do some of those small things which make the nurse's life so tedious. I have repeatedly asked for work, even typing, or at least to sit with some of the English-speaking ladies in labor downstairs, for the hospital is very understaffed, and I know what it's like to try to communicate in a foreign language. All help was refused, however, with the explanation that it had never been received before. Pictures could be hung on the walls which could also be used as screens for an occasional film showing. The hospitals could benefit greatly by encouraging volunteer workers who would be glad to give an hour or two a week to do odd jobs or visit the patients if their work were only recognized. A little appreciation in the form of a badge would go a long way, but alas, that time hasn't come.

A big improvement could be made at the heart of the matter if doctors could lose some of their natural pride in their profession, and their national pride in themselves, and be a little compassionate toward patients. A doctor who appreciates his patients as human beings with dignity, and perhaps even with intelligence, could encourage their cooperation and give them more will to recover. In assuming complete responsibility for their patients, some doctors ignore the valuable self-help that a patient can be encouraged to contribute. I hasten to add that this does not apply to all doctors. My favorites all have that touch of humanness which invariably sends me from them with spirit refreshed as well as body cured. Eventually, of course, psychology in Iceland will extend to all phases of life instead of being confined to methods used in the mental hospital.

After such meditations, the babies are upon us again. Supper follows with bread and butter, oatmeal and milk. Husbands generally visit for half an hour at seven o'clock, the thoughtful ones bringing food and drink to sustain their spouses for the fourteen hours between meals.

Following the evening visit comes the tumult of settling for the night: hair brushing, sponge baths, eating, breast pumps or milking machines (we *are* cows), penicillin shots, laxatives and sedatives. By eleven-thirty, usually, everyone is settled, and the nurses foregather in the front office to drink the fragrant coffee forbidden to us. The lights go out; only one baby, but always one, has insomnia; the green beacon from Reykjavik airport across the street flashes periodically across the room, and we can sneak a smoke if we're bold and the others are willing, for we're sure of no interruption till six A.M.

* * *

After Tryggvi came, my parents wired, "Congratulations. Bring him home so we can see." So three weeks after we'd moved to our large three-room apartment in the west end of Reykjavik, I did take him home, all five pounds of him, in a wicker clothes basket made by the association for the blind. It was a happy trip, and he got fat. Wonder of wonders, he could sleep outside in just a diaper and *not be cold*.

We returned to Iceland in September, and three weeks later I faced my favorite doctor in dismay.

"When do you expect the child?" the doctor asked on my first clinic visit for this marathon. This question makes the patient feel she is on the wrong side of the desk and that the doctor is reluctant to accept responsibility for the whims of nature. The further question "Are you married?" also upsets us foreign biddies until we reflect that marriage after all is an act of law. Such questions as "How are your 'bowls'?" and "Do you ever feel depressed?" provoke giggles or make one glower with suicidal intentions. But I weathered the questions and was disconcertingly healthy throughout this second pregnancy. Of course it would be a girl now, and Mother had sent a darling pink sweater and bootees.

On May 19th of the next year, when Tryggvi was just one year old, I celebrated my birthday by going out on the town and eating all the ice cream I could hold. I ordered a triple helping, in keeping with my American appetite for ice cream, and the waitress served it in three dishes. Baldur was so embarrassed he pretended to be eating one of them himself. There is something lascivious about a very pregnant woman with a ravenous appetite. I waddled home feeling happy and awoke some hours later with cramps. Baldur hurried to the next house to use the telephone, for if the first baby had arrived in six hours, the second would surely arrive in three. He rang the neighbor's bell for some five minutes. The husband would not answer at first, thinking it was some drunk, when it was only Baldur, much the worse for wear. After the third wrong number, Baldur finally succeeded in dialing the fire station.

I was waiting with bag packed, in an attractive poncho-type nightgown with puffed sleeves. Again I was tucked in the basket like a mummy, and we all set off, Baldur in pants and pajama tops, covered with an overcoat, and holding my pocketbook.

No room again at the hospital. I labored in the bathroom, and for the first time saw a privacy screen, separating me from the toilet. Oh well.

Baldur went home, having been given short shrift for coming at all, and fell back into bed. This time I had little inclination to clock anything—only prayed that the baby would be small. The clinic doctor had mentioned the possibility of a Caesarean, but no one on duty knew anything about it. Exactly three hours from the onset of labor, a squealing little boy announced his existence so vehemently that I felt sorry for him. There went the pink sweater. I hugged him, and he immediately went to sleep. Again Baldur was awakened with the glad news. This time the telegram from home said, "Congratulations. Mother will visit you."

And she did, shortly after. We named our second son Ríkardur (Richard).

Our little girl was expected the first of December, some three years later. Good timing, for then I could be up and around again by Christmas. Also Tryggvi was now three and a half and Rikki two and a half. Christmas came and went, and not till New Year's Eve did I have to go to the hospital. This time I traveled alone for Baldur had to stay with the boys. All was in confusion at the hospital—obviously, more than one expectant mother had been moved by the holiday spirit. As I lay moaning by the front entrance doors, the ambulance driver insisted on his fare, which I had forgotten to bring, while the head nurse repeatedly suggested that I go to the hospital in the next town for the baby and that I'd better keep the same ambulance. When I could get a good breath, I convinced the driver that my husband would be glad to pay the transportation fare and that he was the man who had waved goodbye to me on departure, and that there are times when a woman forgets to travel with her pocketbook.

I told the head nurse that where my kindly doctor was, there would I be, and I would cheerfully have the baby on a shelf. I got a well-padded bench in the main corridor for my pains and was contented. Not only could I put my feet on the floor if I wished, but there was plenty of company. Everyone in the world streamed by. A red-haired interne took an interminable history, then retreated while I was being serviced and proceeded to peek at me through the crack in the office door. I hope he took good notes. It was six hours all told before we received our third tax exemption, just within the 1955 limit. He was the 1,652nd baby born that year. Luckily, this time I had bought a yellow sweater set. The telegram from home said, merely, "Congratulations." I was through too.

*   *   *

It couldn't have been oysters, nor a spare pink sweater set, for I had long since given that away. The winter weather of the following year must have had something to do with it. Anyway, when I became pregnant again, I didn't rush out to tell everyone the glad news with my usual impulsiveness, for Eiríkur was still in diapers. I was never so tired in all my life as then. We had a washing machine, but there were three flights of steps between me and the clotheslines, and, of course, three children forever between me and my bed. I telephoned long distance and Mother agreed to come at birthing time; immediately, life seemed brighter.

Late in August, two weeks before she was expected, I polished off a load of ironing in the spare room where Mother would sleep, and that evening we entertained a family who were just leaving Iceland for America. The next morning I went into the spare room for a diaper for Eiríkur, took one look and shut the door. Let it be said that I calmly dressed the older boys and set them out to play before I called Baldur in hysterics. One of the boys had plugged in the iron the night before, and only the concrete walls had prevented us all from roasting during the night. The windowsill was half gone, the curtains were charred frills, and the new steam iron rested on the floor amidst the still-smouldering outlines of what had been our wooden ironing board. The linoleum was ruined and all the clothes were gone. Heaven must have directed us to move out the bookcases a few days before!

For the next two weeks I forgot about being pregnant. We

washed and scrubbed and repaired furiously and despairingly, for though insurance covered the fire, the money for repairs was not given us in advance—we had to repair first and send a bill. There was no money for labor or materials, so a friend in a paint company supplied us with paint, and we supplied the energy. The room was finished the day before Mother came and, though it smelled faintly of paint, she said she had never so enjoyed a visit.

During her first week she helped me mightily, and I rested. The second week a tacit womanly agreement drove me full steam ahead, but with no results. So we agreed that I should walk the sixteen blocks to my next clinic visit. I did and felt fine. Baldur checked out after dinner that night to help build the molds for our new concrete house, and Mother and I pulled out the Scrabble board again. Then, joy and happiness!

So as not to scare the boys with that coffin thing, I called a taxi and arrived efficiently at the general entrance of the hospital. Which door do they carry the stretchers through, I wondered? Inside was one blank door and one POSITIVELY NO ADMITTANCE door. Being a law-abiding citizen, I went through the blank door and sat down in a deserted hall. A man came and sat with me.

"Do you know when visiting hours begin?" he asked.

"Seven o'clock," I replied.

"Are you waiting to visit someone?" he asked, after a few more minutes of staring at my tightly belted, *purple* raincoat (a traffic-stopping color, but it did wonders for my morale).

"No, I came to have a baby," I said.

He had no further questions, so we continued to sit.

After a while I got up and went boldly through the forbidden door. Two nurses drew near and stared.

"I'm going to have a baby. I've been in labor for an hour and a half with contractions now at five-minute intervals," I gabbled.

"Why didn't you come in an ambulance?"

"I didn't want to."

"You're supposed to come in an ambulance. But you can come in and we'll get you ready. It's probably only false labor since you can get around so well."

"Oh, I'm here to stay," I assured her.

"Well, if you don't have it tonight, you'll have to go home in the morning; we're full up."

I got the bathroom quarters again, and a fourth baby boy around ten o'clock. I begged and managed to get an unoccupied private room and there I stayed like a queen, loving every moment. I grew ten years younger in that room, because there was that perfect feeling of knowing my home was in excellent hands, and that the children had a grandmother with them.

CHAPTER FIVE

Anatomy of a House

THE ICELANDIC HOMES BUILT SINCE THE LAST WAR ARE UNI-
formly modern on the outside, ranging from the first un-
imaginative concrete boxes to the present cottage, ranch,
split-level and modern duplex homes. In some cases spirited
designers have poured their whims into concrete only to
have their occupants find them so unsuitable or so incon-
venient that they sell and build more practical houses. The
pity is that other occupants will have to endure someone
else's nightmares, for concrete houses will outlive several
generations and will not be torn down or rebuilt. Today's
designers recognize the fact that since there is no domestic
working class, homes must be built for the housewife to
handle on her own, and now there is a limit to extravagances

and a uniform pitch to staircases.

The contrast between earlier and contemporary concrete homes is not so evident as that between the older shops and stores and the ones being built today. The quaint look of one-story shops beneath cupola-type dwellings is rapidly disappearing from Reykjavik as more and more of these specialty shops are being gathered under one roof in a series of four- or five-floor modern buildings. The "department" store is becoming an established market place though, at this point, each section of the store is usually separately owned. As the supermarket made its appearance some four years ago, corporate department stores may someday replace the presently modern shopping center.

In order to accommodate the burgeoning population in Reykjavik whole sections of apartment houses have been built throughout the city. Unfortunately many of them have not yet been landscaped, and adequate sidewalks and roads have not been put in around them, so they often look like bleak misfits, scattered among small homes and even among farms owned by diehard farmers. Though these new apartment houses have helped solve an immediate problem, there are still too few of them to eliminate the small colonies of Quonset huts left by the British and American armies.

Building a private home in Iceland is very much like jumping into the ocean when you can't swim, just because everyone else is jumping, or because there is nowhere else to go. I read once a story about Henry Ford explaining to his engineers that because of the bumble bee's heavy body and inadequate wings, it was scientifically impossible for him to fly. But, he added, the bumble bee didn't know that; he just flew anyway.

A single house costs between $15,000 and $25,000 to build.

This may not sound staggering to begin with, but the Icelandic homeowners' troubles stem from the meagerness of bank loans. Some people of course have money in the family to start with. We didn't, and our case is typical. One-third of the cost of our $18,000 home (which if sold now would be valued at $25,000) came from Baldur's group security employment pension. (All government and city employees have regular sums withdrawn from their salaries for old-age pensions, and employer groups will lend money from these funds to their employees for building purposes.) A second third of the necessary money for our house came from scattered bank loans, all of small amounts. The last third came from Baldur's salary and, because of this, our house may seem a bit unfinished to American eyes.

Unlike the system in America whereby a single loan can cover the cost of building a house and can be repaid at a standard rate, all our loans are long and short term, so that one month we pay $100 for loans and the next month $200 from our salary of $280 dollars a month. So it has been for the three years in this house with several cost-of-living hikes, two devaluations of the currency and no change in engineers' salaries. Naturally, to help pay off the loans, we are required to take other loans; but theoretically, in time we should be able to get out of the red. After another year or so, we hope that the remaining short loans can be paid off or put on a long-term basis. Then, for the first time in our lives, we will be able to make a budget which includes clothes, doctor's and dentist's bills, entertainment and travel. Up until now our budget has included rent or loans and with the amount left over we pay for utilities and food.

Most private homes today have a large entrance hall, a living room, a dining room (though sometimes this may be just a dining section in the living room), a small kitchen, bedrooms and a bath. All now have back as well as front doors. This arrangement of rooms reflects the customs of generations of Icelanders, but it is changing now because customs are changing.

The living and dining rooms, for the most part little used except by guests, are vast compared to the actual family living space. Here in Iceland the guest has always come first, and the family second—hence the goodies always on hand for guests while the family eats plain food, the best of ornaments and furniture kept in the living room (you never see a painting in a bedroom or a picture in the kitchen). This room is kept immaculate at all times and often locked against children during the day. Though luxuriant with potted plants, this is the one room which has no open books, glasses, knitting, cold pipes, dirty ashtrays, magazines or newspapers. It is a well-tended, empty stage from which it is impossible to determine the personalities of the occupants. Though Icelanders read a lot, there are seldom books in evidence except sets of classic sagas, beautifully bound and often glass-enclosed. (A reason for this may be that bound books are expensive and the paper-bound, modern books are not attractive enough for display.) Lamps are seldom placed or lighted for reading in the living room, nor are the chairs made for family lounging. This is a company room with not even family photographs on display.

The family spends much of its time in the kitchen, where no one but a very close friend or relative is invited. This room is often too small to accommodate four or five people, but being often the warmest room in the house as well as the hearth room, it is the traditional gathering place for family activities.

Until recently, every other house seemed to have blue as its predominant decorating color. Blue was the choice for china both at home and in restaurants, and the popular color for cars. With so much blue inside and blue mountains and ocean outside, I wonder if that cold color doesn't have a depressing effect on the people.

Bedrooms are strictly for sleeping, and only recently for reading or working. The double bed, formerly the size of an American twin bed, is now full size and usually dominates two-thirds of the space. Bureaus are the coming thing, but most people have portable wardrobes or built-in closets with shelves for all clothing which cannot be hung up. There is usually a lamp table, a straight chair and a shelf but, as I say, bedrooms are generally for sleeping. The beds resemble huge puffballs, for the down-filled coverlet cannot be smoothed evenly and must be plumped. Recently bedspreads have come into fashion, but they are still not commonly used because the puff must either be rolled up with the pillow or packed away under the bed or in the closet so that the spread will hang neatly. Incidentally, few Icelanders own bathrobes and often have to buy them when anticipating a hospital stay. There is leisure but not lounging time, and in the mornings adults get dressed for breakfast. Everyone owns slippers, however; they are customary footwear inside the house not only because they are comfortable—Icelandic shoes are notoriously "average"—but also because they keep the house clean and quiet.

Kitchens are kept clean in Iceland. Counters and walls are bare, though it is now permissible to keep a canister set or electric mixer in view. My own kitchens with calendars, cake dishes, memo pads, schedules, wastebasket, always a coffeepot, and usually a dirty cup and saucer in sight do not mark me as an Icelandic housekeeper. Speaking of waste-baskets, these were mysteriously absent everywhere but in offices when I first came. There is little food thrown away in Iceland and, since all paper is imported, there is less need for wastebaskets. Bread and fish were sold unwrapped and paper or bags for other uses were hoarded and re-used. There were no paper napkins, towels, or Kleenex for a long time, and newspapers were too useful to be discarded. Only the fish nowadays is still wrapped in newspapers. Wastebaskets can be bought in many stationery stores now but are mostly accessories in the modern home—there being still not much to put in them.

Every town housewife who is at least forty years old owns a coffee grinder—a pretty wooden box with a crank on the top and a drawer beneath. However, these have been put away for some years now, because of the time involved in roasting and grinding one's own coffee. Americans consider home-ground coffee epicurean, but the Icelandic housewife is glad to dispense with this extra chore. Considering that half a pound of coffee is used daily in many homes, you can understand why. Last summer in the country, where grinders are still used, I hoped to save the housewife some labor by grinding coffee for an hour. I finished with a callus on my finger, two sore knees, and found that what I had ground would barely last the day. She laughed and thanked me any-way.

Despite assumptions, there have never been iceboxes in Iceland, so far as I know. Some have electric refrigerators, but the rest have "cold closets" built into the kitchen on an outside wall or in the storage room with ventilation holes leading outdoors. These keep food chilled most of the winter, but are practically useless in the summer, as one case of food poisoning proved to me. I was very happy when in our third year in Iceland we could buy a refrigerator.

Most town women own an electric iron, and those in a position to collect electrical appliances start with an electric teakettle and mixer, rather than a toaster and vacuum cleaner.

*   *   *

As I mentioned earlier, three weeks after Tryggvi's birth, we moved into a "large" apartment, consisting of three rooms, a kitchen and bath, and an extra room for maid or renting purposes just outside our entrance door.

In the summer this apartment seemed heavenly and spacious. There was no ocean or mountain view, but still we were high in the air rather than buried underground in a cellar apartment, and we could look down into one of the prettiest gardens in the west end of the city, complete with trees more than twelve feet high.

From the kitchen I also had a view of trees, backyards and the spire of the Catholic church. One backyard scene inspired me to write a short story about old people, the only story I've had published in Iceland. And during that and other summers, a melting tenor voice sang arias. I never saw the singer, but learned later that he was one of Iceland's well-known opera stars. As for the Gothic church, many a Protestant thought went winging toward it, mostly in the still nights when I stared through the kitchen window waiting for a baby bottle to heat. Unlike the meeting-type or modernistic Lutheran churches here, those soaring spires on a solid foundation represented home to me and a familiar faith.

Inside our kitchen, which was railroad style, were long,

hip-length counters, cupboards against which I repeatedly knocked my head, no facilities for eating, and a kitchen ventilator that blew instead of sucked. Much as I admire the patience of Icelandic housewives, I think that a few complaints and suggestions from them might have resulted in counters and cupboards measured for the comfort and height of the housewife. The average Icelandic woman, who is several inches taller than I, couldn't help getting a backache at counters like those. With no place to eat in the kitchen, and the dining room having become a bedroom (we parents did not sleep in the same room with the children as is often done here), we had our meals by lamplight in the windowless central hall beside the French entrance doors.

In that apartment we got our fill of cold and wet. It was heated by natural hot water, as most Reykjavik homes are, so we had the privilege of plenty of soft, bluish water, which is good for washing and wonderful for hair and skin; but because of its high sulphur content, it is hard on the silver. However, in summer, although the inside temperature might be in the sixties, the heat was turned off, as is done in many homes. Of course, the winters hit us hard and, after several days of cold, the windows wept with water in the amount of one quart per window per day. This had to be sopped up at least in the mornings and was the first sign of morning activity in all homes without double glass windows, and the reason for the ankle-length curtains favored by Icelanders. During cold spells the water supply diminished and cooled, so that the little which crawled up the hill to our house was only lukewarm. Our mean temperature was 62.5 degrees, often fell to 53.5; and once or twice when the ice was an inch thick on the inside of the windows, it fell to 47 degrees. I have never been so cold in my life.

There ensued a long battle with the landlord to keep on the heat at night. It was illegal to do so, for then there would not be enough for the days, but I confess that several times we did leave it on so we could enjoy a modicum of warmth during the night. The windows were drafty and steamy most of the time, shutting out all views, and the entrance doors were as weatherproof as French doors usually are. I believe there was some insulation in the walls, but none whatever in the roof, and this made our apartment many degrees colder than our landlord's. It was hard on the children as well as us, for they never had a chance to crawl in cotton clothes. They wore woolen underwear night and day through the year and we all wore sweaters in the house.

One night I heard water splashing. I opened the bedroom door and stepped into a hall awash. On this very cold night, the landlord had switched the heating system over to coal, but we had neglected to turn off the hot water system. We opened the trapdoor to the loft and water poured out. Baldur went up in bathrobe and rubbers and scooped eight bucketfuls from the floor of the loft, while I sopped up the hall. Nothing was damaged, though, so we could enjoy the humor of the situation.

These were the nights I used to dream I was in America, sweating in the sticky heat of a 98-degree Boston summer. These were also the nights I saw advantages in eiderdown versus woolen blankets.

The cold preserved the foods in the cold closet, but every cake I made during that season was lumpy because the ingredients never reached "room temperature." Now that I think of it, I suppose this is also why I never had success making bread—it never rose.

Aside from the cold, the only other real problem was washing clothes. In our house, as in many houses which several families share, there was a communal laundry in the basement, three flights down. Ours was equipped with a huge iron boiling pot over a wood fire, several elliptical metal pails for rinsing, and clotheslines. Every third week was mine for washing and, after such a wait, I needed the whole week. I refused to even try the boiling pot, so we got a used wringer-washer. The rinsing pails were on the floor, necessitating much lifting of wet clothes, and since the laundry was generally cold, the allotted week was necessary to dry the clothes.

Scenes from Zola came alive as the ladies set to work in rubber boots and gloves, hair tied up, with semiliquid soap handy and their long sticks. The clothes were stirred in the bubbling pot, and the air was wet with steam. From the pot the hot clothes were lifted on the stick and emptied into the rinsing pails. Streams of cold water kept the floor wet for hours at a time, sometimes all night, as the clothes were rinsed sparkling clean. I was always being advised to boil my clothes before washing them in the machine, but I did as my fathers did. I advanced the theory that with more frequent washing days—hopefully, once every six days—the clothes might need less boiling, but the other women did as their fathers did. Actually, most women do their laundry monthly and do the baby and personal wash in their kitchens or bathtubs, and dry it on radiators. With four children our radiators were always decorated and my temper frayed.

Moreover, one could not dry clothes in the laundry without permission. Eventually we moved the washer upstairs into the kitchen—the epitome of unsanitary conditions. Then, through unusual good fortune, we bought a used automatic washer and dryer at extraordinary prices from a kind member of the American Embassy in Iceland who was leaving the country. The washer was about $62, one tenth of the market price, and the dryer, $124, one-fifth of the going price. Naturally the machines were not quite new, but considering that they cost only one-third of our monthly salary, when the legal exchange was sixteen krónur to the dollar instead of thirty-eight as it is now, this was a windfall. Thank you, Mrs. Knight, wherever you are. I offered the use of these to the other ladies in the house, but they refused, saying that it would make our electric bill too high. The situation was somewhat relieved when each of the others bought wringer-washers a short time later, but still there was friction, for I felt that because my washing took only a day to finish, I could pop in and out of the laundry at any time since it didn't inconvenience anyone. This was frowned on as upsetting the routine and I can now understand why, though I didn't like it. Our mutual problem could have been solved by jointly owning the two machines, but there arises a knotty problem of political theory.

On the matter of buying machines, it is interesting to note that Americans usually spend money first on labor-saving devices to be used behind the scenes, and on family comforts such as innerspring mattresses, whereas Icelanders are more apt to spend money first on accessories for a pretty coffee table and decorations for the living room. In homes having the most modern living rooms, with teak furniture and indirect lighting, the bedrooms may be bleak orphans and the laundry as primitive as the one mentioned. Our bedrooms have always looked better than the living room and were the first finished rooms in our new home in Kopavogur, where we now live. After three years the rooms the guests see are still unfinished.

Aside from the heating and washing complications, life in the west end apartment was not unpleasant. Food stores were nearby and the shopping center and nursery school were only six blocks away. While I had two children, I could always load them into the carriage for trips, provided I wanted to go badly enough. During these years Baldur received a small legacy which enabled us to put a down payment on a car. Baldur found it invaluable, but I got no practical use from it, and car driving is still a touchy subject in our house.

It was during those years that I sank into the routine (though there was nothing organized about it) of housekeeper-mother.

In college I used to dream of mornings when I wouldn't have to get up and could laze and dream until ten. The day has yet to come, for unbelievably, husbands have to get to work in the mornings and often can't find even their socks unaided, though the socks, so help me, are always in the same darned corner of the same darned drawer, undarned. And when the babies come, they operate on their own intolerant schedules, daylight saving time notwithstanding. Ideally, we should have two alarm clocks, one to ring at six, which we can luxuriously ignore, and the other to ring at seven with that "*Now* get up" ultimatum.

Getting up used to mean staggering for the coffeepot, ruminating belligerently about my so-called blessings while the brew bubbled, and downing two cups before that magical feeling arose of being able to cope with the day. After a couple of years, formula, diapers, and dressing and feeding the older children preceded morning coffee. I used to go through whole days without being able to cope with them. I wonder what American mothers do.

In an American family magazine, I saw a soap powder ad showing a "typical" American family at breakfast: Father in his spanking white shirt and arrow collar is drinking orange juice in the breakfast nook; small son, with spanking shirt, is diving into the bacon and eggs, his hair slicked back from clean face; small daughter, in starched dress and hair ribbon, also clean in the face, is hungrily eating cornflakes and bananas. American laundering services and food products are wonderful, so are soap powders, but that scene seemed very unrelated to my life—until I discerned in the background shadows a woman huddled on a tall stool with a wrinkled bathrobe, unmade face and hair in curlers, her sleepy eyes slitted over a coffee cup. God bless that artist for making me feel American again!

When Baldur went off to work, I moved to the windows to mop water if there had been frost, or just to look outside to see if anyone else was alive. From mid-October till mid-March daylight never comes earlier than eight-thirty in the morning and not until ten in mid-winter. A glance out the window told me that the ladies were not only alive but cracking. All down the street, windows were opened to the wind, eiderdown puffs were hung on clotheslines to air, sofa pillows and cushions appeared on windowsills and porches, small rugs hung from balconies, first to air and then to be beaten by women in sweaters. Other women were washing their entries and sweeping their front steps. I gazed at them in admiration and had another cup of coffee.

Meanwhile, the children were off to school, the girls in brown cotton stockings, knitted hats, boots and bright coats; and the boys in mackinaws, corduroy pants and boots, all with briefcases fastened knapsack style on their backs, leaving their hands free and keeping their shoulders back. It snows fairly often in the winter, but it seldom stays long. The warm clothes, especially the boots, are worn against the rains and the wind, which stops blowing between midnight and four in the morning—sometimes.

During the early years I settled the children in their cribs and joined the milk-store brigade. Milk is not delivered, so there was a great clanking of covered milk pails or bottle racks or simply bottles in net bags belonging to housewives buying milk, cream, bread and skýr. (Skýr, similar to cottage cheese and high in protein, is mixed with milk and sugar and eaten as a cereal or dessert.) Milk was sold loose and dipped from enormous covered pails, or it was available in large ginger ale bottles. These one-liter bottles are slippery to hold, but four-year-olds manage quite well with one in each arm.

By eleven o'clock, when the heat was turned on, other people's houses were tidied and clean, albeit a trifle cold. Then the housewives took their bags to the meat store for meat and cheese, to the fish store for fish, to the bakery for bread (if the milk store did not sell bread), and to the grocery store for vegetables and the usual staples. Needless to say, the headache of Icelandic shopping is that nearly every store is a specialty shop.

There is a distinct traffic lull between twelve-fifteen and one, while the nation eats, and the midday news is heard on the radio. Afterwards the men return to work, dishes are washed, floors swept, washed and waxed, special cleaning of one room is done, and a stint taken in the laundry if it's washing week. From three to four is coffee time, either at home or visiting, and then more dishes.

Supper is at seven: a hot meal again, or the remnants of noon meal plus skýr or a thin pudding, and bread. After supper, the day continues for the women with children, but stops for the men while they read the newspapers, listen to the radio and generally relax. Evenings are spent helping school children with lessons, doing handwork (most women have a knitting or sewing project going all the time), ironing or baking. Coffee is again at nine-thirty and more dishes. When the state radio signs off at eleven, the weekday is over.

After such a day, bed feels very good, especially if there are no two o'clock feedings or nightmares to jump for, and if a good book is waiting on the night table.

CHAPTER SIX

A Man Is a Man Is a Man

TO ME, ONE OF THE GREATEST VIRTUES OF AMERICAN LIFE IS the freedom for intellectual companionship between the sexes. Because this is so important to me, it has proved more of a stumbling block in my adjustment to Iceland than it has to other foreign wives, European as well as American.

The emphasis on education for an American girl seems to be increasingly directed toward competition in what is often a man's field: preparing and sharpening the mind, unfolding endless possibilities for exploration in many fields. Unfortunately, the essential difference between the sexes, "equality" notwithstanding, is often forgotten in this emphasis on competition. If women marry and have children, the time and importance attached to a career are quite naturally limited. On viewing the ease with which many wives have adapted themselves to homemaking and motherhood, I wonder whether I might not have benefited more from a thorough training in home economics and nursing.

It seems a fault of American education and society that what one *does* matters far more than what one *is;* we must not only do better than our fellows, but better than our fathers, in a senseless scramble up an endless ladder. During the late 1940's when I was attending Boston University, college girls who wanted only to marry and have a home were considered hopelessly spineless and old-fashioned, and even the most ambitious girls were ashamed to admit they wanted to marry and beget. Though we know from experience and observation that the role of the woman in the home is of paramount importance, it seems to me that little recognition is given this role which requires a combination of tact, flexibility, understanding, psychology, religion, philosophy and compassion (the most beautiful word in the English language), as well as managerial and manual skills and a sense of duty to the community. The efforts of a homemaker take years to bear fruit and a woman can be justifiably proud to have been influential in turning out well-integrated offspring, and to have kept a husband not only contented but encouraged. We should not need to prove ourselves so assertively as modern education dictates but, on the other hand, having had our antennas sharpened into awareness, neither should we have to turn off the whole system and cease receiving and communicating, merely because we have married. To me it seems a tossup—whether it's better to have seen and gone blind, than never to have seen. I can envy the peace of those who adapt with vegetable complacency to housewifery and motherhood, but because I was blessed—

or cursed—with awareness, I must say that my life in Iceland has had more ups and downs. This motion indicates that
at least I am alive and functioning more or less.

Other wives have bewailed high prices and low salaries,
the cost of or lack of amusements, the difficulties of preparing a balanced diet, while my seldom-shared lament has been
the lack of intellectual stimulation and conversation. This
lament has reached such proportions that still, after all these
years, I dizzily anticipate each social occasion, hoping to
kindle a spark of awareness in someone. This rarely happens
at a large gathering but sometimes, in a small group, I can
spend hours listening and talking with no appetite for anything but a cup of coffee and eventually have to be interrupted by my spouse and dragged home. (Luckily Icelanders
keep late social hours, so I don't have to be dragged home
before midnight.) Such an evening of stimulating conversation reacts on me like alcohol. Under its influence, I rarely
remember even the appearance of the people with whom I
conversed, but their ideas and sometimes names remain in
my mind. If I sleep the night at all after rehashing what I've
heard with Baldur, or even if I spend the rest of the night
padding around looking up references and making notes on
the development of some new idea, by the next day that
feeling of exhilaration remains of having learned a new thing,
even so small a thing as a new dance step. I go out as others
do to "have a good time," but it still strikes me afresh that my
interpretation of a good time may be quite different from
theirs.

Armed with a passable education, the aforementioned
curiosity and a frank manner, I expected to plunge into life
in Iceland and to learn all I could about it in the way most
natural to me: talking with people. I expected no resistance

and got none until the glamour of my newness wore off.

In a way it is better for an American woman in Iceland to continue speaking English, for though she may only meet a fraction of the people—the others are unable or unwilling to converse in English—she is at least accepted as being accustomed to talking in mixed groups. Her knowledge of Iceland may be superficial, but she will never retreat and regress until she falls into the mold of the Icelandic woman, who is expected to be ornamental in public, and hardworking in private, and not necessarily intelligent. Men look to men for intelligent companionship and the much-revered "independence of women" in Iceland seems to consist of voting privileges, gained in 1915, and their right to attend dances and nightclubs without male escorts.

Once I began to speak Icelandic, or rather when it was expected of me to behave like an Icelandic wife, I not only lost my foreign prerogative, but most of my comprehension of conversations, even in my own home. The Icelandic language has nouns of three genders and four cases, and an adjective may have 120 forms. Even the gender of a noun can be a stumbling block, for "Hann er fullur" can mean "it (the bus) is full," or "he (the man) is drunk," depending on circumstances.

Now, after having attended one winter at the university in 1951 and some three months at a language school in 1960, I find myself able to converse, but not discuss. As a Danish gentleman once remarked to me: "It's frustrating to have to say, 'Yes, I think so too,' when what you mean is, 'I agree with your attitude but not with your reasoning.'" I used to practice Icelandic with Baldur, but he had already formed the habit of speaking to me in English and tended to overlook my grammatical errors in an effort to understand me.

However, my household vocabulary has become quite large, probably because I have talked mainly with women about their children and homes. My difficulty in discussions is also intensified by the fact that a woman is seldom asked about her opinion on topics of general interest. Usually, by the time I have formed an opinion intelligible in Icelandic, the conversation has veered to another point. So through the years I continued to retreat until I realized with a shock that I was quite unable to talk to men as people without feeling I was "on the make."

My first acquaintances in Iceland were women and I made my overtures to them by asking that unfortunate question, "What do you do?" At that time I was working as resident correspondent for *The Christian Science Monitor*, and so this seemed a natural question to me. But the answer was, "I take care of my home and children."

"But what do you do, I mean, after the housework is over? Do you have a hobby? What do you like to read? What do you like to do?"

The answers were varied: "Oh, the housework is never done"; "I am embroidering a tablecloth or making clothes for the children"; "I like to read fashion and home magazines from Denmark, etc."

What I couldn't understand was that a woman shouldn't also have a vital interest in something totally apart from her life as a homemaker, something for herself as a person. Here again, I assumed that everyone was like me.

So I gravitated to the men who would occasionally switch from their discussions of local politics to such pet subjects of mine as religion or psychology or world political theory. As soon as I joined them, a silence would fall and the conversation would diminish to polite remarks or light banter or, if I was lucky, to resumés of the discussion in one-syllable words which a woman could be expected to understand. Any opinions or questions I might offer on the prevailing topic would be listened to courteously (?) and answered in monosyllables. Baldur would be embarrassed for the men and sometimes angry at me. Finally, when further contact seemed impossible, I would accept defeat and move away, while the men closed ranks and continued from where they had been interrupted.

At one party which we attended, I spent the first hour talking "house" with my hostess and the ladies but then grew restive. It is enough to do housework and be among children all day without going out among adults to talk about it further; and gossip doesn't seem to rate total absorption. Baldur was at the other end of the room with the men and showed no inclination of coming to my rescue. Then fate aided me, for on this rare instance of a formal dinner I was assigned a dinner partner who not only spoke English but was an author and former policeman. A real bonanza!

We talked all through a delicious dinner and sat amidst the guests afterwards still talking as I eagerly pumped him for his experiences. Working with the FBI was one of the career jobs I had considered while in college, but Daddy had told me it was no life for a woman. Here was a man to tell me why it wasn't.

Then I noticed that the women were glancing at me strangely, especially the man's wife, and that the other men had gathered in a knot across the room. My companion did not seem restive so I saw no reason to retreat, as I usually do now. Instead, I tried to draw his wife into the conversation, but she had nothing to say and finally withdrew. I suppose she considered me a formidable opponent but I had nothing to hide, which was precisely the point.

In Iceland appearances are everything. A man may stop and chat on the street with a male acquaintance, but he will tip his hat and move fast if it's any woman but his wife or relative. Lovers meet on the street with blank faces and who is to guess; if they swung hands on the street, it would proclaim their status to this whole small town. So if a woman evinces an interest in a man at a social gathering, everyone supposes that she is starting a flirtation with him—and if she is Icelandic, it may be the truth. Also if a man talks longer than two minutes with a woman, unless he's being interviewed, it's assuredly her *beaux yeux*. Nothing above her eyes appeals to him.

As the drinks were replenished at this dinner party, my companion grew more loquacious and finally suggested we adjourn to the next room where we could speak without shouting, and so I accompanied him unconcernedly. Then began the familiar line: "My wife doesn't understand me." I was startled, but quite willing to discuss man's elemental isolation from his fellows and the possibilities of changing one's attitude toward facts, if the facts themselves are unalterable, but he was not interested in the discussion part. Sadly cheated, I returned to the living room to be met by stares from the women's corner. He reappeared shortly and proceeded to drink himself into a stupor while his wife fluttered about with black coffee and shot possessive glances in my direction. The hostess suggested to me in a tactful aside that I rejoin the ladies. I did for a while, then gravitated to Baldur, my legal and last resort.

"Are you talking about something interesting?" I said hopefully as the circle parted. He smiled indulgently and patted me on the shoulder.

"Why don't you go and sit with the other ladies, dear?"
I threw him a barbed glance, went back dutifully and conversed with the ladies. Who was it who said, "No man is an island"?

I don't know how many parties we have given with Icelandic guests, all or most of whom could speak English intelligibly, when no one, not even Baldur, would speak a word but in Icelandic.

"These people are not shy; they are just rude," I said to Baldur later. "If they can speak English, they should, knowing I don't understand Icelandic, and because I am the hostess."

"Well, after all, they are embarrassed speaking English among each other. It's unnatural for Icelanders."

"What is it for me? I don't like feeling an idiot in my own house. At least you could turn the conversation to include me."

"It's so annoying to have to stop and translate. Besides if you want to say something, you can just speak up."

"Oh, no. I've tried that."

"They're paying you the compliment of treating you as an Icelander," was his final explanation. And maybe they were.

At a recent party a good friend of ours from M.I.T. days dropped in. I introduced him American fashion, that is, by also referring to his line of business as a conversational hook. The others merely nodded, shook hands, and mumbled their own names. The conversation went on around the newcomer as though he was not there. Not a single glance or word was directed to him the whole evening, except that they all shook hands with him when they left. And he was not a social leper; he was just an Icelander newly met. Whether he suffered the agonies I felt for him, I'll never know.

Of course my bad grammar makes me hesitate to speak to people I've just met. As I said, I can chatter but still not discuss in Icelandic, and it seems rude to ask a stranger bluntly, "Do you speak English?" and suffer that embarrassed silence which follows if he does not.

One day Baldur told me he'd be late for supper, but that a man was coming at seven to see him. I was to usher him into the living room, ask him if he wanted coffee and explain that Baldur would be home at seven-thirty. It was all a big mystery.

The gentleman arrived, I did all that was expected, and was careful to speak only Icelandic. What a mistake that was. Unwilling to make baby talk with him to pass the time, I went to putter in the kitchen.

Baldur came, greeted his visitor amiably and closed the door on their top-secret conversation. If I hadn't admitted the visitor, I wouldn't have met him, for Icelandic husbands seldom introduce their wives unless there is some reason.

Half an hour later the gentleman left. As the door closed, Baldur said heartily, "Well, you certainly would have enjoyed talking with him. He's one of the foremost historians of Iceland."

"Oh, no," I groaned. "Does he speak English?"

"Of course. He's spent years in the States."

"Why didn't you tell me!"

"I didn't think of it till now."

"Ask him to come again."

"He's a busy man and I don't have any more business with him."

Sound of fur flying.

The most frustrating of all social outlets, however, is the cocktail party, an American innovation adopted by Iceland to the extent that an abundance of cocktails are served between five and seven on some special occasion. The sexes remain poles apart. One meets, only meets, dozens of tantalizing possibilities, is introduced usually not by name, "my wife" being sufficient, or perhaps merely by a gesture in her direction, and is unable to strike up more than the most superficial conversation. One must not talk shop with men who have come to a party to relax.

"But you talk shop with them. And you never mind if someone talks shop with you," I insist afterwards.

"It's different; I'm a man. It's very tiresome for an authority to have to explain things to an amateur."

"Granted I'm not an authority, only a cut above imbecility, but how can I get to talk with them? I can't make an appointment because I have no business with them."

"I guess there isn't any way. It's too bad," he conceded.

I can relate scores of instances when I have committed the sin of appealing to a man's brain, and I find it insulting to know that a woman is only supposed to bedmake and bedwarm. In this country where husbands often walk a few paces ahead of their wives on the street, open restaurant doors and go through first, it is bad enough to have the combined ideas of the host and hostess passed off as the host's as he sits with the men and she listens hopefully from the women's corner; but the crowning insult is when my spouse listens to some sage's words on the radio, then tells me, who has been saying the same thing for years, "That man really has an interesting approach."

Of course, I married while still in the rarefied atmosphere of college discussions where both sexes participated; and probably many American women who also married during college have found that the scales shifted considerably after marriage and that they have been pushed by convention into women's corners at social gatherings. I agree that many things which men are interested in hold little interest for women, and I am not against male bull sessions or fishing trips, provided I too get permission to get away occasionally from home with other women. Such excursions are pretty rare for women here. Even though a man takes a vacation from his job every summer, feeling he deserves it, he has strong financial objections to his wife wanting a similar trip away from the home and can't understand why she should also need to get away. When a wife does take a vacation, the cost of replacing her in the home equals or exceeds the cost of the trip she makes, and so the husband's vacation solution is for her to get away from it all by camping out in a tent and cooking over a primus stove for the whole family.

To return to my discussion on discussions, I must add that I do not admire the militantly well-informed American women I have known who outtalk all the men in the room and try to force their opinions on them, even though they may know what they're talking about. Aside from these unfortunate offenders, I think that men in America are not surprised to find that women can be interesting conversationalists and may have valuable thoughts. What I object to in Iceland is the assumption that women cannot possibly understand or have any intelligence. This attitude is so prevalent that when an Icelandic man finds himself stranded with a woman, he is obviously uncomfortable if he can't make small talk. It would never occur to him to say, "Do you think this deflation will make any real difference in our standard of living?" By tradition, such topics are confined to conversations with other men, though a man's answer to such a question might be just as superficial as a woman's.

No, this is a man's country in more ways than one, and a woman from another country can sometimes get "queer" after a while. I have blundered and tried again and have learned that, along with the prohibition against male topics of conversation, there are other things which should not be said which I have said:

"You look enough like so-and-so to be her sister." And she was her sister, though outside of matrimony. "Do you only have one child? I thought you had two," was another truly innocent remark, which caused a hasty changing of the subject because there was only one *legitimate* child. And I once said teasingly and carelessly, "Who was that pretty girl I saw you with?" Christmas! It was the "other woman."

Inevitably you get drawn into an atmosphere where every spontaneous impulse is suspect, unless you're drunk. You learn to guard your opinions, adopt a poker face instead of a smile, but stare and gossip for all you're worth. Unless you can remember and conform to all these restrictions, it's easier to just stay home. We usually do.

CHAPTER SEVEN

Cadillacs, Jeeps and Feet

EVERY TRAVELER WHO HAS SPENT SOME TIME IN ICELAND HAS
commented on the amazing lack of class consciousness and
the few distinctions found between classes. Icelanders have
such a strong common heritage that factors which usually
stratify other less-isolated countries unify this one.

Most of them are Scandinavian with a small admixture of
Celtic stock (originating with the first colonizers in 874),
and these people comprise 98 per cent of the present population. Old Norse is their common Scandinavian tongue, retained in almost pure form in the Icelandic language. They
have total literacy dating from 1800 when, through the
strong influence of the State Lutheran religion, such literacy
was required before confirmation. They have a common

heritage of literature and poetry, passed down from the earliest days and still alive and read today. (They publish forty times more books per thousand people than are published in the United States, but fewer magazines.) They have the oldest living democracy, for their representative congress was established in 930 by voluntary agreement of the reigning tribal chieftains. They were welded further together by common suffering and a single aim. There were years of natural catastrophes such as volcanic eruptions, pestilence and starvation, then the tyranny imposed first by the Norwegian king, to whom Iceland signed allegiance in 1261 for aid in enforcing its laws, and later by the Danish crown for almost 200 years until 1854. In their peaceful war against Danish exploitation, the Icelanders' method was patient perseverance and their weapon was education. By 1854 the first break came, because of the efforts of educated leaders in Iceland who insisted on new freedoms for the Icelanders. This break was followed by others, and at last in 1944 Iceland was recognized as a completely independent republic.

With this unifying history and culture, wealth as proof of the quality of a man remains an individual concern rather than a general criterion of success. And under the socialistic system of cooperative and government controls, there is little concentration of money and power among private businessmen.

Yet there are classes in Iceland, the same three as in most countries, but with a very predominant middle class. There are few extremes of rich and poor in Iceland, which makes affluent Icelanders say, deprecatingly, that they are not so well-to-do after all, and the poor ones feel, in truth, that they are not so badly off as the lower classes in other lands.

The "upper class" in Iceland is composed both of those who have had money or influence for several generations and of those who are acquiring or have recently acquired these things—big businessmen, successful politicians, and a few self-employed professionals who have strong political affiliations or whose taxable income is not made public. However, there is no aristocratic class of people which has not only money, but higher education, culture and breeding, for few well-educated people in Iceland make much money and, too often, only the men are exposed to and encouraged in cultural pursuits.

The "upper class" in Iceland seems to be divided into those who give and go to cocktail parties, and those who don't. The first group is apt to be under forty and the other group over forty. Both groups own real estate and/or shares in private businesses. People in the older group often own summer cottages in the country, which some of them may have sold in recent years in favor of taking vacations abroad. Few of these people own riding horses, pleasure boats, more than one car, or membership in exclusive clubs, as most wealthy Americans do, and only a few of them donate their time or money to cultural causes. Both groups take pride in being good businessmen, and hold on to their money in the sense that when they lend money, it's more a case of signing on the dotted line for it.

Among the "non-cocktailers" (and the word "cocktail" is literally translated into Icelandic as "a rooster's tail") home life is conservative, old-fashioned and thrifty. The men drive their own cars, and their wives may have no desire for a driving license. The cars are seldom the latest models, and usually of a conservative color. The wives are well, but not fashionably, dressed and they are shy and kindly. Unlike the second group which spends its money on itself, the "non-cocktailers" sometimes contribute anonymously to public causes. They may take an occasional trip abroad, though it is usually the husband who goes, and generally they use their summer cottage for vacation time. Their children usually go abroad for schooling to prepare themselves for a place in the family business. In short, these people are "ordinary" in a realistic, unaffected sense, and at their social gatherings the men are in one corner and the women in the other.

On the other hand, the "cocktailers" outdo each other in letting their money show. Their homes are extremely luxurious, and whereas the former group buys the best furniture on the Icelandic market, this group will travel abroad to shop for both furniture and clothes. Needless to say, they are fashionably dressed and manage to let you know the prices they have paid for their purchases. When they hop abroad, the wives usually accompany their husbands. For pleasure trips, all Icelanders prefer Denmark, the Paris of the North, where they can speak Danish, the first foreign language learned in Icelandic schools.

Connected as they are with other well-to-do people through business and professional contacts, both groups can buy most things wholesale, or they find someone to bring them tax-free items from abroad, at least cigarettes. However, complaints about the cost of living are loudest among the "cocktailers." They hate to admit they are well off, either because in their own opinion they haven't yet achieved their goal or because they want others to believe they are used to better conditions than what they have. Of course, for income tax purposes, they have every reason to be secretive about their income and to minimize it by complaining. They turn up their noses automatically at Icelandic products, unless they are products of a friend's business; and when they declare preference for an Icelandic product, their reason is that it is as good as the foreign equivalent.

A few "cocktailers" own two cars so that the husband and wife can both drive. Their cars are usually small European ones or big, new American models. These people rarely appear on the streets to shop and have their food sent home to them in bulk; and for any appointment more than a block away, they will drive or be driven, unless the weather is exceptionally fine. Most of them wouldn't be caught dead on a bus and hate to spend money on a taxi, so it is often quite an undertaking for them to arrange to be picked up or delivered.

As for education, their children are usually sent—and they themselves have gone—abroad to study. The boys receive incidental training to enable them to work with their fathers, but they rate more highly their ability to discuss liquors and bars with a knowledgeable air. The girls go to be "finished." The ones who return with considerable book knowledge don't drift with the "cocktail" group for fear that their conversation will be too heavy for the "cocktail" gatherings. However, at the "cocktailers'" parties, men and women do actually mix and talk together.

For entertainment outside their homes, the "non-cocktailers" will attend plays of special repute, but they usually eat at home beforehand and go home right afterwards. The socialites will more likely eat out before the theatre and finish the evening in one of Reykjavik's half a dozen night spots. Almost every class attends art exhibits and every home in Iceland contains from one to a dozen paintings. (The "non-cocktailer" will spend a few thousand krónur, or about $50 to $70, for a traditional landscape which can be passed down as an heirloom, while the "cocktailer" will spend less for abstract pictures that fit in with his own mode of living.)

Though the "non-cocktailers" seldom entertain, when they do, the coffee table is well stocked and beautifully appointed and there is liquor for the men. The "cosmopolitans" would no more dream of entertaining without liquor than refusing a drink without good excuse.

The differences between people are more readily seen here in Iceland where everything is on a smaller scale and one is less limited to a certain sphere, as is the case in a big city in America. Although this "cocktail" group is enlarging, it is not a cross-section of Icelandic life. Many foreign visitors, however, only meet this group and, after seeing their clothes and homes and social behavior, assume that all Icelanders are as well-to-do. Of course, this group is only typical of cocktail sets anywhere in the world. Actually, the "non-cocktailers" are fairer representatives of Icelandic life. Even though they own more things of better quality than the poorer citizens do, they still follow the established customs.

There is a large middle class in Iceland, composed of professionals, small businessmen, skilled workers and white collar workers, and a lower class of unskilled workers and laborers. The middle and lower classes are closer economically than is the middle to the small upper class, while the upper and middle classes are closer as far as education is concerned.

All schools in Iceland are tuition-free and, after finishing elementary school, a young person may choose to go to a special technical, commercial, agricultural, or home economics school, completion of which prepares the young person for a job. Others may go from intermediate school into the high school for further general education plus specialization in languages or science, and then go on to nursing or normal schools, or to the University of Iceland to study theology, law, medicine, dental surgery, philosophy, languages, Icelandic literature and engineering. Many middle and lower class youngsters study in foreign universities, but they do this by winning partial scholarships and working their way through, rather than by depending on family affluence. Because all groups have formal education up to the age of thirteen or fourteen, not to mention the added knowledge gained by many through extensive self-education, differences between classes are not readily apparent. I think I am not exaggerating if I say that eight out of ten male adults on the streets in Iceland are well enough informed about their country's history, industry, politics, and important people, and know enough about geography, fish and wildlife in Iceland to be good guides and competent sources of information for the tourist.

Cutting through the rather superficial class distinctions I have already discussed is a similarity of customs, of the routine daily life, and a moral code uniform to all classes. No one "knows his place" in Iceland and no one is superior and hence not accountable because of his wealth and connections. An affluent businessman will converse quite happily and interestedly with a dock worker, though he might not seek him as a social companion; and a laborer may conduct his interview with a statesman with unembarrassed dignity. This disdain for deference accounts for the absence of any titles for people, except for the use of "Reverend" for the priests. Everyone else is called by his first name, even the president. (This use of first names in Iceland does not mean familiarity, but equality.) It also accounts for the stolid silence which greets the visits of royalty to Iceland, rather than the shouts and cheers which might be expected.

Because of this strong feeling of equality, a fisherman's or farmer's wife can be as proud of her hospitality and table as a lawyer's wife and, up to a few years ago, would more than likely be serving the same foods, though on poorer plates. (Now that more foods are available and life is easier, many women have made a hobby of preparing foreign-inspired dishes. The sale of Icelandic and foreign cookbooks is phenomenal.) Clothes, which might be the most noticeable indicators of class distinction, are in fact poor indicators. Children with mothers who are clever knitters and seamstresses, and there are scores of them, are as well, and sometimes better, dressed than those from well-to-do families. Icelandic women have a sharp fashion sense, once their interest is aroused, and, though some may be dowdy, few dress in bad taste. There are more clean faces and neatly darned stockings than could be found in low-income groups in America and, as in most countries, the poor are more generous than the rich.

Another important unifying factor is the absence of a domestic class. Women of all classes do their own cooking and cleaning, though many employ help for weekly floor washing and waxing, and perhaps ironing and odd jobs. Hired helpers are scarce, however, because girls go to domestic science school nowadays to learn housekeeping, rather than apprentice themselves to a household to learn it.

In the old days, when there was no domestic science school, young girls often worked for a winter in the home of a town relative, where they were treated as part of the family. Today, though female hired helpers belong to unions, they still expect to be treated with the dignity they deserve for the monotonous jobs they do. Anyone who considers treating housekeeping helpers with anything but courtesy and kindness must realize that this good treatment is not "pampering the help." After years of being an unsystematic housekeeper, often physically exhausted from a day of washing, waxing and buffing our thirty square yards of linoleum, I warmly admire someone who can do this job effortlessly and not become annoyed by the children.

Housewives get neither thanks nor payment for their work and cannot help but admire people whose business it is to help them with this necessary, unexciting work. If the "day woman" is on duty at mealtimes, she may eat with the family if there is room enough at the table, or afterwards if she prefers. Every employer invites her hired help for afternoon coffee, sets the table for them both and drinks with her. When she leaves, the househelper always thanks her hostess for the coffee and cakes, and for the day; and the hostess thanks her for coming. Such courtesy is taken for granted in Iceland and extended to every human being. I have always enjoyed and learned something of interest from the ladies who have helped me after childbirth or during Christmas or spring cleaning, and I guess some have enjoyed me, for I have made a couple of fast friends this way whose help I have really appreciated and who I know would unhesitatingly help me out in a crisis whether I could pay them immediately or not. I have never known any Icelandic employee to presume on the kindness shown her, or to expect or accept more than her agreed fee. Everyone has his pride and employees are no exception.

Aside from domestic help, special servants and caterers can be hired for a large celebration, to help behind the scenes, but only at official residences does a "maid" instead of the host or hostess open the door and greet the guests. The basic education which all people receive and the strong tradition of pride seem to have prevented the existence of a domestic class as such, and the nation does not seem to have suffered as a result.

After they finish school, most girls work out in shops, offices or factories until they marry or have children. But once a homemaker, the Icelandic woman seldom has duties outside her home. There is no pressure to engage in civic activities as in America, and good citizenship for an Icelandic housewife means taking care of her family. There is no parent-teachers group in which women are expected to participate, nor are they expected to be den mothers for Cub Scouts. There are various church-aid groups which make and repair vestments and of course choir groups, but no social societies associated with the church. One's churchgoing habits are a personal affair and do not reflect on one's standing in the community. As might be expected, elderly people of all classes attend church most regularly.

Recreational facilities for golf, swimming, skiing and ice skating are available to all classes; but the most popular form of recreation seems to be the summer vacation in the country, and any family which is able visits a summer cottage or inn, camps out in a tent, or simply drives out on sunny days for picnics, berry picking or potato harvesting. (Though this is too small a country to support such traffic, one out of every nine persons owns a car or truck. Bicycles are seldom used except by children.) The unlucky families who don't have country relatives to welcome their children send them to summer camps or let them work on farms. This close connection with the land is one which Icelanders recognize as

valuable, and it keeps the realities of country life from becoming a memory to urban dwellers.

Each summer, especially when the herring catch is good,
there is a rush of girls and women to the coast villages for
well-paid work. Middle-class girls may also do summer work
in factories but return to school in the fall, whereas lower-
class women work in the food and clothing factories or the
spinning mills full time. Anyone is free to better himself by
gaining free higher education; it is merely a matter of choice.

A young Harvard student, unwittingly a "Peace Corps"
pioneer, worked in a fish factory here as an odds-and-ends
man. He not only learned enough Icelandic to encourage him
to take a degree from the University recently, but learned
an amazing amount about fish and Icelanders. He was surprised at the quality of discussions ranging from poetry to
government which these fisherfolk engaged in, and rated
them as first-class people—Icelanders in the realest sense.
And he may be right. I've had little opportunity to be around
fish, and though I now like to eat them, I still cringe at
decapitating and cleaning them. For "real" people, I'll put in
a bid for the farmers and those who come from the country.

I've quite forgotten to mention the "notables" of Iceland
who rank with businessmen and politicians in notoriety but
are far less well paid. These are the painters, such as Jóhannes
Kjarval, and Jón Stefansson; sculptors such as Ásmundur
Sveinsson and Sigurjón Ólafsson; poets such as Davíð Ste-
fánsson, to mention only one of many living poets; and
writers such as Guðmundur Hagalin, Gunnar Gunnarson,
Kristmann Guðmundsson, and Halldór Laxness, who received the Nobel prize for literature in 1955 and whose
book, *Independent People*, was on the Book-of-the-Month
Club list for 1946.

Of all groups I have met, the artists are the most refreshingly original in thought, the least hidebound in behavior, and the least concerned with or affected by politics. The good ones *are* as revered as statesmen, as Baldur told me long ago; but honor cannot be eaten. The state awards them insignificant sums from time to time, and some have received preferred building sites in recognition of their fame; but most of them have to take extra jobs to augment their income, and many of them are forced to live as the poorest people do.

For their benefit I would love to see an art festival week established in the summer, during the tourist season, so these artists could reap well-deserved rewards. One or two weeks of exhibitions in all display windows as well as exhibition halls, open air concerts in the parks, chamber music concerts in the flourishing nightclubs and museums and libraries, poetry readings in the coffeeshops, meet-the-author gatherings in the restaurants would be as exciting as June 17th, Iceland's Independence Day. Such a festival would bring kindred souls together and help generate an atmosphere of spontaneity and enthusiasm sorely needed in Iceland. These unofficial "statesmen" need to come into their own.

CHAPTER EIGHT

Country Boy

COUNTING OVER THOSE I KNOW WHO HAVE STUDIED ABROAD, I
have decided that there are three kinds of men who choose to
settle and make their living in Iceland. I won't consider
those who have never been outside Iceland and have little
desire to go, and who therefore stay here as a natural course
with no question of choice.

The first group are those who train abroad in specific
fields such as business and plant management, fish process-
ing, construction and electrical engineering, and advanced
medical and law training. (This last field has great potential,
for most of the prominent men in politics are lawyers.) Because of the steady business expansion of the last twenty
years, men in this category can be assured of finding a niche

for themselves when they return to Iceland.

The second group are those who have studied or worked abroad and return to Iceland to settle with the assurance that their relatives' financial or political connections will enable them to get good positions and make a comfortable living. The prospect of being a big fish in a small puddle is very appealing to anyone, and Iceland is a small puddle, or rather a small land surrounded by a very big puddle. Icelanders who have been lured away by the glamour of foreign countries and have lived abroad often feel that they become submerged nonentities, even though they may be earning more money abroad than they would have at home. Usually they return if only to visit and, if they don't, they keep their contact with the homeland through newspapers, magazines, letters and contacts with all Icelanders living in their locality.

In this country where almost everyone is related to someone else, where genealogy remains the only topic to rival the weather, there is great satisfaction in knowing one is a vital part of the community. As it is impossible for an Icelander to be anonymous in Iceland, so it is impossible for him to feel he is quite alone or forgotten. I maintain that a person in Iceland will never starve, not only because most Icelanders still know how to grow potatoes, but because there is always some member of the family to help out.

The third kind of Icelander who "goes out," as they say (reminding one inexplicably of a person released from prison), and comes back is the kind of person exceedingly rare in these days of self-interest—the old-fashioned patriot, the man who loves his country despite its faults and whose whole interest is directed toward developing its assets for no personal rewards, but for the good of the country. In

this group can be found idealists who are also egotistical
enough to expect rewards for their services, and who are
aware to some extent of the advantages of political affilia-
tion. But there are other idealists, practical in the impersonal
economic sense, who look upon this land as a vast undeveloped potential. They are hopelessly dedicated men who
live and breathe their work, who are sweetly unconcerned
with financial rewards, and to whom the term "country boy"
means neither an uneducated yokel or a member of the
farmer's party, but an ICELANDER in the fullest sense, and
in large sweeping capitals.

I married one of the latter specie and hereby offer my
handkerchief for the tears of all wives of dedicated men,
who seem to be out of this world most of the time. They are
the queerest, most unpredictable, most exasperating, most
unreliable and forgetful, and at the same time the kindest,
most optimistic and most admirable kind of people a wife
cannot small-talk with.

But Baldur is living proof that such men can become somewhat domesticated. He who was unacquainted with coffee
making, baby changing, baby burping, floor sweeping, and
fastening necklaces on women (?) has now become an expert. He who used to mash down my newly baked cakes to
test their surface tension, used my best knives for screw-
drivers, my chamois duster for a paint rag, and the dish-
towels for cleaning the floor or his shoes, now does none of
these things. He who used to pace the entire house while
thinking, leave mounds of sticky pipe ashes in every ashtray,
drink the *last* bottle of milk religiously before going to bed,
keep the radio at high volume, and fade into an absentminded haze in the middle of a sentence hasn't changed
one iota.

But he who would not lift a finger to repair or renovate, who seemed all thumbs at carpentry, who took no interest in gardening, suddenly decided after seven years (it does take a while for changes) that the time had come to build a house, though he had more ambition than money. This perennial procrastinator built us the house of our dreams: dug the foundations, helped build the molds for concrete, insulated it, and for the most part painted it inside and out and laid the linoleum in every room. (Icelandic homes have concrete floors covered first by linoleum and then by carpets as the budget allows. Only the rich have wood floors.) All this was done in the time usually allotted to "resting" from office chores. Since he had always objected to emptying garbage and washing dishes (His tender advice was: "You just lie down now; you can do the dishes tomorrow"), he solved the problem neatly by ordering a dishwasher and garbage disposal unit, on the theory that we might as well be hung for a sheep as a lamb. (We're still hanging, by the way.) Who would have thought he would change so! Then he leveled our rocky lot singlehanded and sowed grass. Trees were a passion with me but have become a madness for him. Other husbands may look sheepish over a mysteriously lipstick-stained handkerchief, but mine looks foolish when I discover yet another seedling protruding from his parka as he creeps into the house. Now we have *only* seventy-one trees on our 90-by-110-foot lot!

Yes, husbands are wonderful inventions of society, and I think every girl should have one of her own. Mine has the additional asset of an excellent knowledge of chemistry, which saved me from danger on one occasion when we were still in our rented apartment.

One rainy Saturday my restless eye discovered that Tryggvi's panda was grey and black instead of white and black. Heavens, what filth, I thought. (We all have that reaction some time or other, though the object may have needed cleaning for months.) I ran a sink of water, put in lots of Icelandic chlorine to bleach the grey, and lots of concentrated vinegar to keep the black color fixed. Immediately bubbles formed, thin steam arose, and I began to feel woozy. I called Baldur from the next room. Before I got half through my garbled explanation, he threw open the kitchen window, unstopped the sink, pushed me out of the kitchen and slammed the door. While I groped for a chair in the hall, he ran through the house and opened every window.

"What's the matter?" I gasped.

"You made chlorine gas. How do you feel?"

I was surprised at my ingenuity, and then angry at the chlorine manufacturers for not saying on the label that you mustn't mix it with vinegar. But then, I admitted, maybe not everyone would think of mixing them.

Half an hour later I retrieved the waterlogged panda, now brown and grey, and with my breath held I rinsed him and guiltily hung him by his ears in the laundry. (It wasn't my week.) He stank and, for the several days it took him to dry, I covertly examined the other ladies in the house, praying they would not be poisoned by his body odors. Nothing happened, though, and, come to find out, it *was* my washing week after all and I had missed three days of it.

Baldur introduced himself to a laboratory while in his early twenties—late, you might say, but Iceland had just emerged from a severe depression by 1940 and was beginning to expand its fishing and small consumer industries. When there was still no prospect for the growth of chemical industries, playing with chemicals was not a poor country family's idea of finding a secure job. After hatching some definite theories and some near-hazardous explosions in the laboratory, Baldur joined with two schoolmates—one now a successful businessman and the other a mathematics teacher—and created a small factory for the production of carbon dioxide from limesand, quantities of which were available from seashells thrown up on the coast. This experience led him to do further research on the subject later for his bachelor's thesis at M.I.T., a work well acclaimed by the chemical engineering department.

Recently I enumerated for a friend the various projects on which Baldur has worked as an employee of the Icelandic government. After naming five projects without explaining all the work they entailed, I realized that such a bare account made one wonder just what he had done with the rest of his eleven or so years working as a chemical engineer.

To begin with, he had no work at all for six months after our arrival in Iceland, except for odd gas-analysis jobs he was offered now and then. He searched and questioned among the existing businesses and found no place for his ideas. There were only two research organizations dealing with natural resources: one connected with the University was doing work on chemical analyses of various materials and employed only chemists at the time; the other was the government's State Electricity Authority, which employed a number of engineers but worked mainly on electrical communications, power projects and hot-water heating for homes. There was nothing much here for Baldur.

His mother visited us and castigated him for not getting a respectable, "secure" job—in a bank, for instance. He owed it to his "rich" American wife at least to support her, she told him. She was right about his finding a job soon, for we were living almost rent-free in our little attic through the goodwill of his sister and her teacher-husband. (Iceland boasts of its literacy and educational facilities, but pays its teachers salaries equivalent to those of factory workers, and its professors only a fraction more. Teachers in Iceland can't strike, and can only resign, which they are doing in increasing numbers.)

After listening to his mother, Baldur's spirits plummeted, but I, childless and idealistic and not at all concerned with gracious living, castigated him myself and reproached him for losing faith in himself. Luckily, through the years, we seldom fall into depressed moods or even become sick simultaneously. Thus one could always pull up and help the other along when necessary. In this case he took fresh courage and continued his search for a job.

By greatest good fortune, the director of the State Electricity Authority proved to be both farsighted and optimistic, and agreed that it was time for Iceland to consider expanding its research activities. He too found the idea intoxicating that one day Iceland might be able to have thriving chemical industries of her own, rather than spend millions of krónur yearly to import even such a necessity as salt. He created a temporary job for Baldur and gave him full rein for his ideas, though he could not promise much money for the research nor guarantee that any promising project would be developed, since he himself was but a government employee. Thenceforth began Baldur's love affairs with Iceland's natural resources.

During our second year in Iceland, we went north for a summer work-vacation and settled in a spotlessly clean, very hospitable hotel named Reynihlio. This hotel on the banks of Lake Myvatn, some three hours' drive from Akureyri, was a tourist mecca, offering boating, excellent trout fishing in the lake, steam baths, yummy food and bathing in an underground cavern in a natural hot water stream. It was also not too far from Dettifoss, one of the largest waterfalls in Iceland. The hotels at Myvatn attract bird specialists from all over the world, geologists and tourists interested in the weird lava formations left by old volcanoes, and mining engineers interested in the mineral mountain area where Baldur was to work.

As soon as we arrived at Reynihlio, I hung on the wall of our room a calendar brazenly entitled "A Chapter a Day" and started work on a novel under the best conditions a would-be author could envision—nothing to do but write, eat and sleep.

After inspecting "my world," Baldur drove me in a jeep to see his. Up and down winding roads we bumped, past the old steambath house, past open stretches of lava, pausing only for a band of wild horses to flee across our path, manes streaming in the wind, unbridled bodies gleaming gold and chestnut and white. We slowed at the top of a hill and looked down into a strange land of reddish mountains, their slopes festered with craters. Thin fingers of steam rose soundlessly from the depths of these craters and, as we descended into the valley, we saw pools of bubbling mud. It was horrible and fascinating. All tales of witches' brews and landscape of the moon sprang to mind, as did a clear vision of my high school chemistry class, for the air was full of that unmistakable odor of rotten eggs.

"Sulphur. Doesn't it smell good?" said Baldur, sniffing appreciatively as we got out of the jeep.

The sulphur I saw then didn't impress me, for most of it was underground, mixed with the natural hot water and steam which rose so endlessly from the fissures and the roaring boreholes. Baldur's problem was to recover the pure sulphur from the mixture, and to do this he invented an apparatus. He patiently explained the details of it to me, which I forgot but when I saw the results of his labors, I was impressed —his sulphur was a shining chunk of pure chartreuse yellow, a heavenly color for an evening gown, I thought.

It took several summers before this real sample of sulphur was given to me, however, for plans had to be approved, cost estimates made, an experimental pilot plant set up, and makeshift equipment collected to make up for what the budget didn't include. Well, Baldur patiently completed the project, but shortly afterwards the market price of sulphur fell and further development of the project was shelved.

Several years later, Tryggvi swallowed a piece of my sulphur sample when he had a severe cold. When his cold symptoms disappeared the next day, I remembered the old sulphur and molasses remedy used in America. Sulphur is potent and tricky stuff—especially if you're absentminded. During one of those first trips north, Baldur sat on a hillock to meditate about his drill holes. By the time he was ready to leave, he felt a distinct draft on his backside. Sulphur fumes from the unnoticed steam fissure had disintegrated three layers of pants and stained him green—temporarily, thank goodness.

At about the same time as he was making this investigation on extracting pure sulphur from steam, Baldur noticed that Lake Myvatn was filled with tiny organisms called diatoms —microscopic, one-celled algae which floated in the lake in greenish-brown patches. Baldur knew that the bodies of some of these algae sank into the mud after death and disintegrated, leaving silica shells which when dried and purified are useful and inexpensive for filtering all kinds of liquids, even beer, for instance. Although this was not his mission at the time, he decided to find out as much as he could about the kinds of diatoms existing in the lake and the quantity of the deposit. He never talked about it with me, though, so naturally I was upset the day he returned from a long field trip with somebody's nylon stockings tucked in his bag.

I had returned home a few weeks previously from the production of our second son (a womanlike method of calculating time) and was looking on as Baldur unpacked his duffle bag. After the usual articles to be washed, he drew out a bundle of white parachute silk which he tossed at me.

"I picked it up along the way. It's good nylon. Maybe you can make something of it."

He drew out another bundle—puckered pink nylon, two meters of it. This was also something he'd picked up.

Then he glanced quickly at me, hesitated, and drew out a pair of used nylon stockings.

I fastened my eyes on my sewing while an unexpected lump formed in my throat. True, I had been out of commission for some time since Rikki's birth, and husbands are known to stray. I hadn't suspected this of Baldur, but he was still staring at the stockings as though he didn't know where they came from.

"Well," I said lightly. "Did you buy those for me?"

"I bought them for Algy," he said (hard *g*).

"Who?" Never trust a man left alone.

"You know—algae. Remember? The little green things in the water?"

I hiccupped with laughter while Baldur looked rather hurt.

"No one could make up a story like that," I sighed finally.

"I didn't make it up. It's true," he insisted, with complete lack of humor. "I bought the pink cloth to make a bag to use as a sieve, but it was too porous, and so was the white. Then I thought of the stockings and they worked fine except that they were too long, and I hated to cut them since they were so expensive. But when I skimmed the algae off the lake, they stayed right in the toe of the stockings," he continued, tossing them to me. "Just wash them out and you can wear them. They're your size." (He never did bill the office for that two-dollar pair of nylons used for "research" —perhaps he wasn't sure they'd understand either.)

I think that is the only laugh Baldur has had over those tiny creatures whose corpses are so important to the world as chemical filters. After he had completed his tests on this, his second undertaking, and presented his findings, there apparently arose the feeling that the idea was too good to be true, especially since it had cost practically nothing and since Baldur didn't even have the dignity of a fixed position in research so he could be termed an "expert."

The project was delayed and forgotten by everyone but Baldur, who continued making tests. Finally, after five years, the government called in foreign experts to decide. To everyone's surprise but Baldur's, the experts confirmed the value and accuracy of his findings and suggested large-scale investigations. However, these confirming reports took three years to arrive because few scientists dare to submit their precise data and conclusions until they have written them in language so cautious and qualified that they are of no interest to the layman and a headache to the breezy reporter who tries to summarize them. (Hollywood script writers have never captured that atmosphere of mutual horror and anticipation felt by the participants in a scientist-reporter

Our house in Kopavogur — plenty of space for children.

Reykjavik with a view over the lake. (*Photo by Vigfús Sigurgeirsson.*)

Even in a new bus, a trip through the country is an event. (*Photo courtesy Timinn, Reykjavik.*)

Akureyri is a pretty town. (*Photo by Vigfús Sigurgeirsson.*)

interview.) Nevertheless, late in November, 1960, the government sent Baldur to Holland and Germany to seek information about producing and marketing diatomaceous earth. He returned with the assurance that Iceland's deposit of this material was the largest in Europe and could command a ready market. Now, in July, 1961, plans for setting up a small, experimental plant by next summer are on the horizon.

Baldur's salt project has been received with a similar lack of support. Because there are many mountain streams and rivers, Iceland has no need of fresh water from the ocean, but salt is another matter. Almost 90 per cent of Iceland's exports are fish and fish products, and much of the fish is salted. Great quantities of salt are imported regularly for this and other purposes. Because most of Baldur's work has been in connection with natural steam or hot water, he devised a plant to extract the salt from seawater by heat from piped natural steam. (The temperature of natural hot water in some sections of Iceland is as hot as 154°F.)

Despite the fact that salt is an inexpensive commodity relative to other imports, and that Baldur's method would have been slightly more expensive initially, it seemed for a time that the plan might have success. The government even called in two experts—one from the United Nations and the other from the U.S. Technical Assistance Division of the I.C.A.—to check Baldur's methods and calculations. These gentlemen added their authoritative support to the project and suggested further investigations, but then there ensued a muddle of red tape and conflicting interests which has not yet been untangled. Work on the project has been suspended for the time being, but the production of salt from seawater may eventually be instituted, if only as one of several products which can be extracted from the ocean.

Having been brought up on a farm, Baldur could appreciate the eternal problem of trying to make enough hay during a short, wet summer to feed livestock throughout the
winter. Because he was interested not only in the elements
contained in natural hot water but also in its uses, Baldur
designed and submitted drawings for a hay-drying machin-
ery, which used piped hot water as the drying agent. Unfortunately, someone else's idea to use imported oil as fuel
for heating and drying the hay met with more success, and
this method is now being used in at least two new hay-drying
plants. Being an inquisitive woman, I asked why expensive
imported oil should be used when cheap hot water is available. The answer was that most European countries who
dry hay artificially use oil and that it was therefore a more
familiar process. Naturally, I then insisted on knowing why,
if the government decided to use the familiar, more expensive
method initially, it didn't also make plans to develop the
hot water idea to reduce future costs as speedily as possible.
There was no answer to this question.

However, one of Baldur's fond dreams has become a reality, for during the last few years he managed to convince
all concerned of the value of having a research lab attached
to the office for industrial-chemical experiments. To our surprise, the lab was actually built and is operating successfully.

Most of the difficulties in getting chemical industries
started in Iceland stem from the modern practice of spending only for quick rewards. The government seems more
interested in the hasty increase of consumer goods than in
the development of any new chemical or other industries
for future prosperity. The return from investing in research
does not seem quick, and in this socialistic democracy there

is little private capital available for investing. Progress is made by measures which are supported by the government, which means that any successful business venture must be backed by one of the parties in power. Strong party affiliations can be very valuable, and it will be interesting to see how much progress, if any, can be made by scientists who are politically independent.

Every time another of Baldur's projects was suspended or when those of political favorites received the priority I thought he deserved, I would discourse on the hairline which separates admirable "persistence" and blind "stubbornness" and wonder whether Iceland held any future for either of us. I quite agreed with him that scientists and artists ought to stay out of politics, but I had problems of my own. I was trying to take care of four children in an economy plagued by strikes, price increases and currency devaluations, and I was still receiving rejection slips for my short stories. As a transplanted American, my American scenes had no modern validity. American editors were not interested in stories of Iceland and I could not write well enough in Icelandic for my books to sell here.

At these times Baldur's dedicated spirit should have wilted, for he got little encouragement from me. Now in July, 1961, the engineers have finally gone on strike. Is he discouraged? Not at all. For this long overdue "vacation" he took another loan, bought paint, and has almost finished painting the outside of the house single-handed. He's unquenchable.

CHAPTER NINE

I'll Pay You Tomorrow

IF AMERICA IS BECOMING A LAND OF CONFORMING INDIVIDUAL-
ists, I think it can be said that Iceland is still very much the
land of individual conformists.

As America strives more and more to achieve cultural and
material uniformity, the individual seems compelled to per-
sonalize his house with unique landscaping, colors and
fences and himself with a hobby, the more different the
better, in an effort to separate himself from the amorphous
anonymity which surrounds him. Sometimes Americans seem
to live as the Pueblo Indians—in stratas composed of cubbyholes of behavior and ideas.

The Icelanders still begin as individualists and are proud
of it. They gather each with his own opinion which he vigor-

ously defends, but then they often end up doing what the majority does or doing nothing at all; they possess the intellect to form their own opinions and the courage to assert them, but often they lack the will to defy conventions enough to change them. This shows up in city life especially, where yesterday's pioneers have become today's inert upholders of the status quo. However, this passive attitude does not extend to politics, for whereas American non-voters are usually those who are too indifferent to vote, the percentage of Icelanders who do not vote refrain from doing so purposely because they don't agree with the platforms of any of the parties. But these non-voters all *care,* and though I can't prove it, I have the feeling that each non-voter when questioned could explain exactly why his own philosophy prevented his voting. Ninety per cent of the Icelanders voted in the last 1959 congressional elections, a fair average when compared to the 85 per cent who voted in the last U.S. presidential election (which percentage I believe was higher than usual). But this great interest in politics is not wholly due to the smaller and more compact size of Iceland.

This is the original "no comment" country, where it is impossible to stage a rally or start a movement. American play producers who for years have tried out new plays in Boston ought to try them out in Reykjavik. Here the producer will find an attentive, interested audience which will always respond with polite applause, but he won't know whether he has a hit or a flop. It is not that efforts to arouse the audience are unappreciated, but that each person is determined not to let himself be swayed by the emotion of the moment, and would rather go home and mull over the play, idea or speech before arriving at a conclusion.

This independent attitude is especially evident in the

business world, where it is nearly impossible to get anyone to commit himself to an agreement when first approached; you must return tomorrow or the next day or the next to see whether he has decided, and if you don't approach him repeatedly, nothing will be done. Similarly, there are few written contracts between employers and employees, but rather verbal agreements, the terms of which are carried out according to each person's sense of responsibility; and these agreements are as binding as a written one would be. Most Icelanders feel it unnecessary to make a man swear to anything because the implication then is that his word cannot be trusted, and they are very trustworthy people once they have agreed to a bargain.

Though this assumption of trustworthiness is diminishing somewhat with the development of a sharper business sense, one can still lend money freely to a friend, provided he asks, and be sure of being repaid. An Icelander has too much pride to ask help from another unless his need is great, nor does anyone offer help for fear of offending pride. But if an Icelander asks for a loan, it means he has no alternative and he may not be refused except for good cause. There is no written contract, but the lender may say he will need to be repaid in six months, or the borrower may say he can repay it by such and such a date. When the time is up, the borrower either pays without being reminded or makes a point to explain why he can't pay yet. But he usually pays—even at the risk of borrowing from someone else, which is a real loss of face. If a loan is made for an undetermined period, the borrower pays it off as he can, and there is no shame whatsoever attached to his owing money to someone, nor does that friend ever mention it, with one exception. If the lender suddenly finds he needs the money, he notifies the borrower and the borrower is duty-bound to repay it at once.

At the time I came to Iceland, this assumption of mutual honesty was much in evidence in the shops when one might not have enough money with him to make some purchase. Almost always one was told to take the purchase along and complete the payment next time he was in town. If it was more than a small sum, he could still usually make the purchase but had to leave his name and address. This may sound like a bad business method, not to haggle over money, but it worked, and naturally no one made a purchase he didn't really plan to pay for.

Nowadays the race for money is so acute, and in cases I know of, goodwill has been so abused that the former unsuspicious attitude has been replaced in most shops by a pay-as-you-buy system, quite impersonal and easier on the bookkeeper.

I try not to buy on credit, for my memory is notoriously bad concerning money. (Whether a figure has three or six zeros following it is all the same to me. I am only concerned about whether it's a lot or a little money in relation to my pocketbook. I can understand and appreciate the comparison that our new house in Iceland cost the same as five new, small cars, but even Baldur can't make me remember how much a car costs. I'm more apt to remember impractical things like visual impressions, gestures or voice inflexions or the family tree of Henry VIII—don't ask me why.) So when a sales person offers to let me pay later, I either refuse and decide wisely that I really didn't need the item at all, or dash into town with indigestion the next morning to pay what I owe, terrified that I might absentmindedly betray this admirable trust invested in me.

Although there is little installment buying here except for

such items as furniture, one may pay for an article over a
period of months and take it home when it is paid for. This
system is much easier on the nerves than wondering if you
can meet the next installment. In this painless way we acquired six silver coffee spoons and forks, which we couldn't
have afforded outright and would have postponed buying
indefinitely.

Everyone is tolerant about money problems and seldom
is the electricity really cut off, though after one written and
one phoned notice, the telephone may be disconnected. The
telephone bill is about the only utility bill sent through the
mail. Instead bill collectors go around on foot through rain
and snow to take a chance on finding people at home and
able to pay. This seems an inefficient method to me, but it
does keep the collectors from becoming sedentary and allows
a personal contact. (After two years of opening the door himself, striding in and reading the electric meter, our meter
reader now rings the doorbell first, then smiles, tips his hat,
and asks for permission to read the figures. This disconcerting change in behavior is quite pleasant and thrills my mid-
dle-aged heart.)

One day when Baldur was at work, a collector came with
a bill owed by a chemical organization in which Baldur was
a partner. Because the man had driven some six miles out
to us in Kopavogur, a service charge of twelve krónur (then
seventy-five cents) was added to the bill. The man didn't
mind that I couldn't pay the bill, but insisted I pay the
service charge.

"I'm sorry, I don't have it," I replied in Icelandic.

"Now, I can't believe that," he said, making my temper
rise. "Surely you must have twelve krónur in the house."

"Well, I don't. I have two empty milk bottles which the

children could cash, but that wouldn't be enough." And it was true. It happens not infrequently at the end of the month that all pockets have been emptied, my piggy bank, and the spaces deep in the upholstery of the chairs. Also Baldur holds to the custom of paying all utility bills himself, the assumption being that one needs experience in handling money and that women are notoriously bad managers.

"Well," said the man, "this is a matter for the police. We'll have to ask your husband to come to the police station to settle this. How will you like that?" The children stood beside me gaping.

To this day, I still haven't found the Icelandic equivalent of "You can't get blood out of a turnip," so I merely stared at him resentfully, wondering what the police could do that he couldn't. Finally I said I'd call Baldur on the phone and let the collector issue his summons directly to him.

After he had carefully removed his rubbers on the porch, I let him in and called Baldur's office. In less than a minute his angry outburst to Baldur dwindled to stammers and pauses. He hung up and turned to me incredulously, speaking now in English.

"It's true," he said. "You really don't have it."

"That's what I said."

"I'm sorry. I just couldn't believe that anyone wouldn't have twelve krónur." Obviously we are not typical Icelanders.

I ushered him to the door, feeling too angry to speak.

"Where are my rubbers?" he asked. "I left them here."

Eiríkur, my second youngest, broke from the cluster of staring children and said, "I know where they are." He hopped down the front steps, gingerly fished the rubbers out of a mud puddle and presented them to our guest.

"I'm so sorry," I said, my mouth twitching uncontrollably.

"It's all right, all right," he said and, holding them by two fingers, went down to his car while I smiled benignly on Eiríkur.

Nevertheless, when Baldur was late coming home that night, I anticipated a call from the police saying he had been detained. Not Baldur. He came home grinning. He had stopped off to pay the twelve krónur and had been invited in for coffee and cakes, for it was not Baldur, but the treasurer of the company who should have paid the bill.

My encounter with the impatient collector from the chemical company has had no equal. On the contrary, another collector from a fire insurance company came four times to the house to get his money. The first time I didn't have it and he said he would return in a few days, but didn't. When he did come back again, I didn't have any money for him. The third time I did have it, but he had no change. When he came the fourth time and got paid, I felt as sorry for him as he did.

This casual attitude toward bills is not confined to the day-to-day business people transact with local stores and companies. A foreign exporter who had business with an Icelandic import firm a few years ago made the sweeping comment that Icelandic importers are notoriously unreliable, that they import goods according to unwritten agreements and, when the goods arrive, they do not accept them on the pretext of having no money. In cases where the goods were made especially to Icelandic order, they could not easily be resold and the exporter (who finally sold his product to the importer who had ordered it originally) had to await the pleasure of the importer to get his payment.

If the exporter's claim is true, it does explain the fact

that Icelanders among themselves are much more tolerant about money matters than are businessmen in other countries. I believe the truth of the matter is not that the Icelandic importer is intentionally deceitful; it is just that he so often juggles and invests his money in various enterprises, that he can only hope that the required sum will be available when the bills come due. In the fishing industry, one may make 100,000 krónur in a season whereas another, not so lucky, makes only 10,000. It's always a gamble, and so the fishermen and the merchants engaged in exporting and importing think in terms of big money and the big chance and have no feeling for a relatively steady and dependable income. The farmers, on the other hand, have an attitude about money much closer to that of large industry, but modern Iceland's economy is based on the elusive herring rather than farming.

Truly, Icelanders are among the kindest people I know, and there is real sympathy behind their stiff exterior. A man will give you the shirt off his back if you ask for it. He will not offer anything, however, and is often intentionally impersonal.

Though I was quite accustomed to American pressure salesmanship when I came to Iceland, I've only seen it in action here in connection with representatives of Jehovah's Witnesses. In the shops, salespeople never used to smile (they sometimes do now), were barely courteous (they are more so now), would sell you the article requested but never offer a substitute if the article was sold out. Some of the glamorous young salesgirls still say, "Ekki til" (literally, "It doesn't exist" or "We don't have it") without bothering to flutter their eyelashes in search. If you want it enough to withstand the stares of the other customers, you can insist that what you asked for is directly behind her on the shelf, and she will hand it to you with not a flicker of discomposure, take your money and saunter over to the next customer. This can be especially annoying when it is an American product. One woman repeatedly tried to buy ginger ale and was as repeatedly told that it was "ekki til" when she knew it wasn't. Finally her husband solved the dilemma by asking for "ging-ger-ali" (with hard *g*'s) and got it of course.

I have decided though that it is often better to let the value of a product speak for itself than have the salesman run the risks incurred by talking too much. When we took the children to the States in 1955 for a five-month stay, a salesman selling dishes rang my doorbell one afternoon. Enchanted at this door-to-door service which is nonexistent in Iceland, I listened to the young man, looked at his dishes and began to count my pennies. Then he caught sight of Tryggvi and Rikki playing close to the door.

"Are they yours?" he asked.

"Yes," I said modestly.

"They certainly are cute kids," the young man said admiringly. "Your husband must be very good-looking." After this damning statement bristled in the air, nothing more was required. He packed up his dishes and left.

One day, back in Iceland, I went shopping in a furniture store to look for a desk. (Baldur had asked me what I wanted first in the way of furniture and I had specified, "a desk of my own.") I saw several I liked in the store, but there was no one around to wait on me. I coughed a few times, said "Hallo," and felt like a fool. Then a man in shirtsleeves stuck his head around the doorway from an inner room.

"What do you want?" he asked. (Icelanders can be very

direct.)

"I was thinking about buying a desk," I began.

"Five thousand krónur," he replied, without advancing.

"Thank you," I said as his head disappeared.

The price was not exorbitant for those times and, because he was an Icelander accustomed to his countrymen, he probably felt that I would buy it if I liked it and could afford it, but that I wouldn't do anything until I had gone home and mulled it over. And he was right. Though I felt at the time that he could have pulled out the drawers and shown me all the tempting cubbyholes, I must say I love being allowed to make up my own mind about a purchase. As it turned out, we finally got a desk from another shop, but it was "my desk" in name only and finally became "the desk," in which I had half the storage space. Baldur obviously had more paperwork to do than I, who was only writing a book, and besides, who ever heard of a woman needing a desk? While reflecting on this situation, I realize that there are actually few things anyone *needs*. Most of my stories have been written at the kitchen table with their author wedged in a baby's highchair. I can't say that a desk would have improved the quality of my writings, but perhaps the quantity, for highchairs have their limitations.

Another interesting difference to me between Icelanders and Americans is the generally tranquil attitude of most Icelanders. You can't argue with someone who merely listens and says, "Well, well," while considering what you say. You can't become passionate about the need for vital changes in the school system when your listener says mildly, "That will change with time," and will only discuss the issue after you have simmered down. When a volatile woman flies into a tempest, her husband will not repeat, "Yes, dear; yes, dear," in an appeasing way, for this would imply that he agrees with her. Instead he is quite willing to sit motionless and let the words flow past and express the hope that she feels better after her outburst.

Husband-wife quarrels *do* occur among Icelanders, I've learned with surprise, but if guests arrive in the heat of the fray, the host and hostess will drop their quarrel and with convincing sincerity say, "Will you pass me the cake, dear." Only after the guests are gone will they resume their fight. And are voices raised between parent and child? Never. The parent does not lay down the law, but expresses his opinion, and the child either obeys or quietly disobeys according to his own sweet will and without fear of punishment.

But the Icelanders themselves have circulated a joke about their placidity:

One man approaches and hits another.

"What?" says the victim. "Are you going to hit me?"

The attacker strikes again.

"Are you hitting me?" inquires the victim, now slightly ruffled.

The attacker hits the third time and finally the victim hits back.

On the street a woman falls down, someone drops an armload of parcels, two schoolboys roll on the ground, one throttling the other until he is blue in the face, children shove their way to the front of a queue, or a man far back in the queue demands service as he feels he has been waiting long enough among the women, a child darts into a store and steals an orange—and no one stops to "interfere." But let a baby cry in its carriage and everyone and his brother stops to talk with it, jiggle the carriage or remark disparagingly on the absent mother who didn't dash out at the first whimper. Once when Eiríkur was crying in his carriage down in our front yard, an old woman entered the yard and climbed the three flights to our apartment to inform me. I thanked her and felt duty-bound to rescue him immediately, though I had known he was hungry and wanted to cool his formula first.

Taxi drivers will seldom open doors for you, nor will anyone help ageing people across a street, and a husband (not mine) will sit at his leisure while his heavily pregnant wife lays a table with goodies she has stood hours baking to serve to half a dozen guests. But this is not callousness to the Icelander. He knows that others have the same pride in their self-sufficiency as he, and he will do nothing to help you—unless he is asked.

A member of the American Information Service in Iceland summed up her short visit to continental Europe by saying, "In England, they look down on us as barbarians, but they hold out their hands for tips. In France, they hate us and soak us. In Italy, they fawn on us, give us extravagant service and triple the price. But I'm glad to be back in Iceland. Maybe the Icelanders don't give anything, but they don't ask for anything either, and if they do something for you, it's because they like you."

CHAPTER TEN

Skál!

A FEW YEARS BACK, A FRIEND CALLED TO MY ATTENTION A TRUE story she was reading from the old turf days in Iceland. It was about a farming couple who had suffered through a winter of extreme privations. After the spring slaughtering, the farmer found he had a little money left over, money not needed for the bare necessities (and they were bare!). Naturally, this extra money belonged to him and, as naturally, he rode into town, bought himself a bottle of local spirits and proceeded to guzzle himself to the ears. When he came home, rather the worse for wear, his wife merely noted without rancor as she looked up from her scrubbing that this was man's way, and that after he had slept it off, he would return to work as usual.

My friend said, "How understanding that woman was to know he needed a chance to forget things and not to resent his drinking." Was it understanding or resignation, I wonder?

"He could have asked her if she'd like a new dress, or bought her a new washing kettle or some good food for both to eat. Couldn't he?" I argued. "At the least he could have given her nips from the bottle and had a grand drunk with her."

Nope, when a man earns money, it's his. He apparently feels acutely the responsibility of supporting a wife and family, and at times he needs a chance to forget his responsibilities. But after he has paid for the necessities of life, his wife can presumably scramble for her own accessories, or she may be able to coax an allowance from him to spend as she chooses. What generally happens is that from the household money she is free to save as much as she can for herself, provided, of course, that everyone is well fed and satisfied. (The results of a discussion group of Scandinavian women in Europe a few years ago showed that, of the four countries represented, only Icelandic husbands doled out the food money daily or even bought the food themselves—not for the wife's convenience, but in order to handle their own money—whereas the other women were given stipulated amounts weekly or monthly and could shop as they liked.) In Iceland a man feels very strongly that his extra money is his because he has earned it. Presumably his wife has not earned anything.

Of course, in the old days, the man actually did bring home the fish, and hard and dangerous work it often was. The farmer, however, had the bacon, or rather the mutton on the hoof in the back field and could knock off one at will for the cooking pot. But his arduous work was gathering the sheep from the grazing fields, shearing and slaughtering them, scything grass and making hay—all necessary monotonous jobs done under variable weather conditions. His wife naturally shared a lot of his work by helping with the haying and milking the cows and nursing the sick animals. This work was done in addition to making her own bread and butter, in addition to her usual three meals and two coffee hours, her washing, ironing, scrubbing, mending, sewing, etc., all done under primitive conditions. (Ten years ago one of my friends had a hand-crank sewing machine on which she sewed miles of material. Foot treadles were and are still everywhere. I have one and still have no motor attachment.)

It is true that life in Iceland has fewer stresses than in larger countries, but this situation seems to be changing rapidly. As in any other country, it is not the fishermen and farmers and those engaged in physical labor who find it difficult to relax, but those who spend an eight-hour day in an office who regularly come home exhausted. By tradition, men may not dissolve their tensions in tears as women can, and nowadays it is not needful or fashionable to split a tough piece of kindling as was done in the early days of every country. We have to think up our own methods of relieving tension. Baldur lets off steam by taking long walks, working on the house, going on field trips or painting pictures. (One of his best oils was done when he was furious.) I work off mine by scrubbing walls, beating cakes or, best of all, by writing stories, poems or essays, whichever suits the mood. Stresses are emotional, but we know they can be relieved by physical activity, and sometimes even cured, for the physical diversion often changes our attitude toward the problems, and therefore eliminates the strain. Blame our modern so-

ciety for depriving us of the physical outlets that so often
relieved our minds and enabled us to sleep at the end of a
day with both body and mind tired.

Iceland still has many such work outlets for women, but
not for men. Modern life is here to stay, however, and Icelanders who formerly only went on occasional binges now
accept the cocktails-before-dinner importation with pleasure.
Americans *always* drink cocktails before dinner, they tell me.
It is the mark of the cosmopolite to be able to discuss brands
of liquor knowledgeably, though drinking in Iceland is
mostly done for the results, not the taste. Icelanders are
either drinkers or teetotalers, with very few moderates.

I must say that I enjoyed drinking far more in America
where it was regarded as incidental to a gathering instead of
the *sine qua non.* Here it seems so many parties are spoiled
and so much pressure exerted to drink in a group to show
friendliness (I'm friendly even sober). We simply dare not
ask certain people to visit because without the liquor, which
we cannot afford and seldom buy (except when one of us
takes a trip and can buy it tax-free on the plane), the party
just goes dead. It's bad enough that whiskey costs $6.00 to
$7.00 a bottle, but when you add the price of soft drink mix-
ers, which we only buy as a treat for the children at Christmas, and consider that the guests will not leave till the bottle
is empty, this amounts to a costly evening. It makes you wonder whether people really come just to see you. A pleasant
evening for one person may mean drinks, noise (Icelanders
are very quiet except when they have had a few drinks),
and lusty singing; for another, drinks, noise and flirtations;
for others, good food and gossip; and for conservatives like
me, good conversations and just something to eat.

In this town of Reykjavik where everyone has shed his

rural individuality for an air of hesitant, apologetic imper-
sonality, appearances are everything and a man exercises his
male prerogative by going out with the boys to drink. Anything he does at that time is forgiven (if his driving license is
suspended for drunken driving, he can even choose the
season of the year when it would be most convenient for him
to be without a license) for he has the good excuse that "he
doesn't know what he is doing." His wife will lead or follow
him home, tuck him in bed and not reprove him; he can
always count on her for that. And while under the influence,
no zany antics are discouraged, But if a man, cold sober,
rides down a hill on a sled with his kids, builds them a snow-
man in the yard or plays ball with them, he's considered
"queer." I've seen no such "queer men."

Times are changing in respect to some social gatherings,
however. School reunions used to include only classmates,
not their spouses, though the class might be co-ed. Girls who
have received a higher education seldom marry. (See Chapter 14.) The reunions were often biannual events with an
overnight trip to the country where plenty of liquor was
served. Office parties and trips also used to be strictly for
employees, to the joy of the single girls who have no qualms
about married men. A number of husbands were not reluctant to take their wives, but shuddered at having to question
the unbroken custom that had prevailed for years. Icelanders
do not stick their necks out, so in this circumstance, the men
merely found excuses for not participating. When it was discovered that they would participate if wives were invited,
the wives were asked.

This reunion and office-party business was a sore point between Baldur and me for years. I've missed every one of my
own class reunions, and hated to be excluded from his if

there were to be women present. I could appreciate that the wives of class members would not fit in, but yet Baldur was hurt that he was not included in the one college gathering I attended in America. And, no doubt, if I had joined the newspapermen's organization in Iceland, he would have felt the same resentment as the wives of the newsmen would have felt at having me there.

At the organization dances—the annual ones that each professional or non-professional work group holds—there is more sobriety than there used to be. These used to be a three-hour dinner with cocktails, speeches, wines and songs, followed by a dancing period during which the men sat and got stewed and the women merely sat. Now, in some cases, the dinners have been speeded up, the speeches shortened or eliminated, and more time given to the dancing. Most people actually dance now and only a few groggy souls try to outdo each other with sidesplitting inanities.

Icelanders pride themselves on "finishing the bottle." This is probably due to the fact that until recently liquor was not served in public places, but was available only in bottles bought from the State Liquor Monopoly. Whereas most Americans stop when they have a glow on, the Icelander is not so easily misled. Almost compulsively he stays to finish the last drop, so that an informal party may break up at five in the morning. If anyone has a liquor addiction, it will no doubt be intensified when he comes to Iceland, for here he will never want for drinking buddies and will suffer no lack of respect from his neighbors because of his drinking habits. And if his drinking interferes with his job, he can be sure that even the boss will be indulgent.

Among Scandinavians, I believe Norwegians are supposed to hold the record capacity for alcohol. Once at a party a young Norwegian attempted to prove this: "I can drink any Icelander under the table. *Skoal!*" So it began. Cautious Icelanders never make such statements, they merely attend to them. In this case, after an hour of steady skoaling, the Norwegian, almost green by this time, collapsed in sobs of shame on the table, while his Icelandic companions went on drinking as usual, and his wife hurried with the coffee. Icelandic wives are not teetotalers as a rule, but even the party-girl wives know that someone has to get up in the morning to fix breakfast or dress the children.

Icelanders are unfortunately so shy that only by drinking can many of them relax and be friendly. Now that light drinking is becoming more fashionable and more public places have liquor licenses, the urge to get blind drunk is not so prevalent.

Because I was used to drinking water with meals in America, I found it difficult to adjust to the wines which are generally served in restaurants here. (Though the water is tops, you have to insist to get any, and you're considered a "hick" if you don't drink the imported wines.) Being the sort who drifts peacefully into sleep after two highballs, I am often irritated at being pressed to "have another" or to "Skál" only and every time everyone else does, preferring to sip at my own leisure.

One night at the home of a charming couple who had several interesting guests, including us (?), our host strongly urged me to sample his choice wines "to improve the flavor of the food." I thanked him and demurred, saying I hadn't finished my pre-meal drink yet. (Because I'm such a skinflint, I still can't discard a half-full glass or a half-smoked cigarette just to be sophisticated). He kept urging me, saying that liquor improves the flavor of the food. This I could not let pass, alas.

"If alcohol dulls the sense of taste, as it says in the medical books, how can it improve the flavor of good food?" I offered. "It should only be served when the food is hopeless." (And that food was good.) But I shouldn't have said what I did. Everyone looked uncomfortable and the joy was gone from the drinking. Someday when all is forgiven and the host realizes I was not trying to demean his food but defend myself, perhaps we'll be asked back, for I have seldom enjoyed an evening's conversation so much as that time.

Since I have dealt at such length with the drinking problem in Iceland, one might assume that Iceland's consumption of spirits is phenomenal. It isn't. Compared to some European countries and the United States, we can see how low Iceland's per capita consumption really was in 1960.

France drank 21.7 liters per person; Italy, 9.2; Switzerland, 8.4; West Germany, 6.1; England, 6.0; United States, 5.7; Denmark, 3.7; Sweden, 3.8; Norway, 2.3; Finland, 2.1; and Iceland, 1.7.

Obviously, it's not always what you do but how you do it that can be offensive.

Aside from the drink-to-the-dregs habit, which is more a custom than a disease, there have been noticeable strides made in the last eight years toward helping the alcoholic in Iceland. Alcoholics Anonymous has its counterpart here in Iceland, and is run exactly the same way as in America, with the striking difference that its members are not anonymous to one another. The original director of this organization explained that in so small a country anonymity would be impossible. This exception doesn't seem to have harmed the organization, for it has spread with the years, and now includes help for women drinkers as well as some instruction for close relatives of problem drinkers. It has its own hospital (for men, at least), as well as a farm in the country for convalescents.

The perennial suggestion for decreasing the drinking problem for everyone is to brew a beer stronger than the 3 per cent type available now. At $3.00 per bottle for the least expensive local liquor, one can believe that it takes a lot of no-how to resist getting drunk, as another bottle might be a long time coming.

CHAPTER ELEVEN

Neither Fish Nor Fowl

MY INITIATION INTO THE AMERICAN WIVES' CLUB TOOK PLACE A
few months after our arrival in Iceland. Its title is inaccurate
for in the first place it is not a club, but an unofficial gathering of all interested American wives of Icelanders, having
neither purpose, dues nor officers; and, in the second place,
it was originated fourteen years ago by two Canadian
women, one of whom is still here.

After I had spent those first few weeks in Akureyri among
Icelanders, trying to express myself in elementary words, I
felt as though I had a great deal to say when I joined the
club. And at the Wives' Club, there was plenty of opportunity.

Icelanders have sometimes referred to the club as the

American Gripe Club, forgetting that whenever Icelanders are abroad, they invariably forgather to exchange their impressions of the country. We do just that, much to our edification and peace of mind.

Our stories are surprisingly alike: The girls, all of middle-class families, met their husbands while they were in school or training in America. Though our first view of Iceland is generally favorable, there shortly begins a period lasting several years in which we wish we had had our heads examined before agreeing to come. The food, housekeeping methods and general way of life all come up for bitter criticism, in about that order. Then follow comparisons of in-laws; the language difficulties; morals; and upbringing of the children; and for those not domestic or willing to be absorbed in the details of domesticity, the struggle between the sexes. After such broad observations on the difficulties of living in Iceland, interest turns to the more practical matters of how to cook the food in question, how to knit with the Icelandic untwisted wool without it shredding, and where to find picture hooks, curtain rods and steel nails for concrete walls. There was no hardware store when I came and the dime store, American drugstore, and supermarket were sadly lamented. (There are still no dime stores and the drugstores are just apothecary shops.) One lady had the good fortune to dream she was in a supermarket, had eagerly filled countless baskets with vegetables, fruit, etc., only to awake when she reached the checking-out counter. (Probably the black market vs. legal currency exchange problem disturbed her fantasy.)

Although the climate is a standard opening for conversations among Icelanders, I don't recall any of the wives doing more than commenting on it, one reason being that there is no formal ritual to our meetings, and the other that the damp, chilly weather is here to stay, and there's no use talking about it beyond advising wool instead of nylon underpinnings to avoid kidney troubles.

In the beginning, the Wives' Club gatherings were sit-on-the-floor ones with simple refreshments. Gradually they have changed to more formal occasions, for living standards have continuously improved, and we have become older and more Icelandicized and do not sit on floors. A few brave souls, generally those newly arrived, have offered spaghetti or hot dogs for "coffee," but eventually we all come to accept and expect open sandwiches, cake and cookies at ten o'clock.

A real family feeling exists in the club, which accounts for the regularity with which it meets in the homes of its members, and the desire to limit it to those who really are permanent residents in Iceland. There is a great exchange of maternity clothes (some one of us fifteen is always pregnant) and baby furniture (when it was hard to get) and practical help for those with problems. Since the husbands all work in diverse fields and have little in common, the monthly meeting is often the only time the girls see one another. I say "girls" though we range in age from twenty to seventy; at a guess, the average age is thirty-five.

From our curious position of being neither fish nor fowl, we get a bifocal view of life which is interesting, though confusing. We hear from Icelanders that, since we are foreigners, it is best to be Norwegian, next best to be American, and worst to be Danish. From European men or Icelanders brought up in Europe, we hear that Icelandic women are cold and without charm, that they are more appealing than French women until they open their mouths, and then the French women's rating soars, every time. We hear that Dan-

ish women have little beauty but much charm. From Icelanders in Iceland we are told that German women (in Iceland) are aggressive and bold, that Danish women are
superficial, and that American women will tell you the inti-
mate details of their lives when they first meet you. (I argued, and successfully, about that last statement, saying
that if we talkative Americans didn't speak up, there would
be a funereal silence for the first half hour when strangers
were first introduced. I didn't add, though, that many Americans hate a silence whether an angel is passing or not.)

After being here a few years and settling into the quiet,
conservative role of a housewife in Iceland, I can sympathize
with the newcomer from America who bursts in with an
almost terrifying vitality, and begins an enthusiastic barrage
of questions or admiring comments, usually in a hearty positive voice (I say "positive," for the very inflection of Icelandic is diffident, almost humble), and I feel sorry for his
confusion when a gaping silence falls. On the other hand, I
can sense the embarrassment felt by the Icelanders in this
same situation, who are overcome with shyness and unable
to speak and unsure about how to answer the American's
questions.

We comment with amusement on the American tourists
who flood the city periodically each summer. They come,
the men with their cameras and cork soles and the women
with mammoth satchels, sensible shoes and a busy, inquiring
air. A tourist couple passed me on the street one day and
their words floated back: "The natives here look just like the
people back home. Imagine!" Another took a picture of
what he exclaimed to his friends was a "typical Icelandic
girl." She is pretty too but, regrettably, an American and
the president's daughter-in-law at that. Another tourist

pleaded for "just one picture" of a genuine handknit sweater a child was wearing. The American mother didn't have the heart to tell the tourist that the sweater was from Macy's, New York.

The Wives' Club seems a staid and stodgy group at first but, after a while, most of us look forward to its meetings as a time when we can let down our hair. Visitors sometimes come, but none so keenly appreciated as someone's mother, whom we welcome as our own.

Three times since I have been here, the club has expanded to include members of the American Embassy because certain club members have wanted to revitalize the club with "real" Americans who would "bring us up to date" on American life. Each time, after half a dozen meetings, the girls begin to regret this expansion. Aside from the fact that there are often as many wives attached to the Embassy as are usually in our club, which makes the meetings too expensive and large for many of us to accommodate, we find that our permanent status gives us little in common with Americans who are here temporarily and for a different purpose.

Truly, the Embassy members have overwhelming problems in acquainting Icelanders with the American way of life, problems that divide their interests from ours even as they divide their interests from Icelanders.

Usually new Embassy members will spend days, weeks or months at the Hotel Borg looking for a suitable apartment, whereas we move in with relatives in a pinch. Because of their heavy social obligations, they need a larger apartment than most Icelanders, and they want private laundry facilities. It is expected that there will be more wear and tear on the apartment rented to transients, so Embassy people often have a long wait, and are charged the highest possible rent when they find a place.

When an Embassy member tries to make friends through normal channels, he finds it very difficult. His children, through whom he might meet neighbors, are educated within the Embassy, not in the Icelandic public schools; the Embassy wife will do all her shopping except for milk and fish at the Keflavik commissary on the airbase. There will be little opportunity, therefore, to shop with her neighbor even for clothes ("I can't afford to buy clothes in Reykjavik; the prices are too high," one Embassy lady announced), and naturally they do not eat the same foods. Although most Icelanders have some reading knowledge of English, few prefer to speak it so, aside from the Icelanders most frequently contacted by the Embassy, it is a matter of luck to run into those who can and will speak English.

Ordinarily in America, people make friends through churches or clubs. Churches are not well attended here, despite the growing number being built, and Iceland has no clubs for leisure life. The transient status of Embassy couples also slows acquaintanceships, for most Icelanders hesitate to start friendships which will necessarily be terminated in two years, and Embassy members lack the time to cultivate a leisurely friendship with these reserved people.

As I mentioned before, Embassy wives who visit the Wives' Club find many of the same obstacles there that exist in their relations with Icelanders.

The resident wives, as Icelandic citizens, are subject to the same exorbitant customs duties and food purchasing problems as the Icelanders. They operate generally on a much lower salary than Embassy members, have no help in the house, much less a "maid," and no entertainment budget. Food problems are often acute, and what may seem deplorable conditions to an Embassy wife may seem quite enviable to a resident wife.

One Embassy lady recounted her anger at having received a twenty-five-pound turkey for Thanksgiving when she had distinctly ordered a fifteen-pound turkey from the commissary. (I've yet to meet anyone in Iceland outside of the Embassy or Keflavik who has been able to obtain a turkey at any time, though there is a small turkey farm near Reykjavik). Another lady lamented the fact that she had received a case of apples when she had ordered oranges. (This I heard at a time when no fruit at all had been available for months on the local market.) It is difficult to know how to reply to this sort of a complaint! One lady suggested that for efficiency purposes in baking cakes, I buy half a dozen cake mixes (at $2.00 per box), take one morning off from housework (who is to take care of the children and have dinner on the table at eleven forty-five?) to mix them up in my electric mixer (no mixer), bake and frost the cakes, and freeze them in my deep freeze (no deep freeze). Then, she added, I would never worry about not having a cake ready when guests arrived. I appreciated her goodwill, but couldn't think of a way to answer without sounding like a poor relation. Furthermore, oblique references which Embassy wives may make to "the natives" are keenly felt since all of our husbands are "natives."

The resident wives too have problems because of their status. Those married before 1951, almost half of us, acquired Icelandic citizenship automatically upon marriage, but still retained American citizenship because they did not bear arms for Iceland, work for the Icelandic government, etc. Those married after 1951 have had to attain Icelandic citizenship through residency, but have still kept their American citizenship. However, the latest stated policy of the Embassy was that it represents America to the Icelanders, not America to the Americans. The Embassy does not recognize our dual citizenship of course. As a result, every summer a chill spreads through the club when the Embassy holds its Fourth of July celebration and the resident wives are not included unless their husbands happen to be of interest to the Embassy. Since the American Embassy in Paris does not follow this policy, nor does the Icelandic Embassy in Washington on its own Independence Day, the American residents find it unreasonable, and especially galling when Icelanders who were invited ask about their absence.

My connection with the American Embassy in Iceland has been favorable, but seldom close, for despite the knowledge that the resident Wives' Club has been recommended as a liaison entry into Icelandic life for Embassy members, the Embassy itself has done little to endear America to the American residents. Aside from notices to keep up our registration as citizens, I have never received either notice or instruction as to how to cast an absentee ballot for elections or as to whether I was eligible to vote at all. Thanksgiving Day and Christmas have a more passionate meaning for us transplanted Americans than for those to whom such celebrations are just another of a series of dutiful entertainments, but there is no one to blame for that except the North Atlantic ocean. And as mentioned before, the July Fourth celebration does not include residents as a whole, though Baldur and I have been asked for the last three years. As a recent Embassy official said, "We will help you if you are in trouble regarding your legal status, but we recognize no other obligations toward you"—an understandable explanation, certainly, but not guaranteed to make one shout three

Prayers by the bishops precede the opening session of the Alping. (*Photo by Petur Thomsen.*)

Saturday night dance. (*Photo courtesy Timinn, Reykjavik.*)

Following sheep roundup, the farmers claim their property. (*Photo by Vigfús Sigurgeirsson.*)

A modern farm with local church in southern Iceland. (*Photo by Vigfús Sigurgeirsson.*)

cheers either. (Icelanders always shout four "hurrahs"—I had thought three was a mystic number everywhere.)

Embassy members have complained, however, that their time is so heavily scheduled with parties for the same people that they have little opportunity to strike out on their own and make friends. I hope this complaint is sincere, for the Icelanders often feel that the desire of Embassy members to visit Icelandic homes is not always genuine. It is the Embassy's job to "entertain" and "be interested in the people," but after two years the staff members are transferred elsewhere, for Iceland is considered a "hardship" post. Are they *really* interested in the Icelanders as people?

It seems to me that Embassy members could get to know Icelanders best by working with them and among them. Sending American children to Icelandic schools creates an unnecessary problem for the Embassy children, but food shopping in local markets would provide a good and instructive common ground. Rather than have an Icelandic instructor teaching Embassy adults the language at the Embassy, I feel Embassy members would be more in contact by attending schools in Reykjavik which teach the language to foreigners or by taking the University courses for foreigners. If Embassy members had fewer social obligations, those who wished to pursue private hobbies such as lamp-shade making, weaving, painting, music, cooking, or some particular sport, could thus receive instruction with Icelanders interested in similar things, and they would find their language understanding growing by being instructed in these hobbies in Icelandic. Compulsory instruction naturally would be a burden to anyone, but it should be a welcome relief for those talented people who wish for free time for further pleasurable studies, to have a chance to forget themselves and be themselves. After their stay in Iceland, they could feel they had gained something for themselves as well as having created a bit of goodwill among the just-as-important lower echelon of the country by having been genuinely interested in something other than "diplomacy."

"This country is really nationalistic. I've never seen so many flags in my life as in Iceland," someone said with amusement. Yet, except for the British, no one *talks* more about his country's superiority than the American. "You know what's wrong with your country? It's ———"; or "If I were an Icelander, I'd set up a nice little business here in such and such a line and really clean up"; or "Yes, you have a nice little country here, fine principles. You just need a little push"; "Yes, I'm proud to be an American. Best country in the world." Such openings as these do not elicit enthusiastic response from the Icelanders. But unlike Americans in America, who would bristle if the U.S.A. were criticized so freely, the Icelander, who is always considerate of the opinions of others, listens reflectively. But *he* believes his country really *is* fine and doesn't feel the need to say so. And he doesn't want a push from anyone.

Again, many Icelanders feel, and rightly so, that they and their wives are invited to official Embassy parties for business reasons. Americans in America often entertain business connections in their homes. Icelanders do not entertain in this way. The business customer is seen in the office or taken out in public for lunch. If it is necessary for the customer to seek the businessman at his home, the wife is not included in the meeting, and if she does serve coffee, she is not expected to be introduced. An Icelandic guest of the Embassy, there-fore, does not feel it necessary or fitting to return a business invitation of this sort, and certainly not in his home. He feels even less obligated when he knows the Embassy members have an entertainment allowance for cultivating friends and that the foods and wines do not come from the host's own pocket.

An Icelandic woman generally cleans and bakes a lot for guests. This is her way of showing her welcome, and the guest is complimented and complimentary. But it seems not a fair return somehow when her American hostess returns the invitation by offering, on a silver platter, cake from a cake mix. In this colder climate, Iceland's caloric consumption is higher than that in America and most of western Europe, and dinner without potatoes and bread is empty fare indeed. Finely appointed dinner tables with silver and candles and flowers make little impression unless there is filling food.

It seems that Embassy men and women who like sports and are genuinely interested in the language, men who like philosophy or political theory, men and women who enjoy art and music, and women who like sewing, baking, and all the old-fashioned, housewifely skills have a better than even chance of enjoying themselves and really getting to know Icelanders. But the well-dressed socialites will inevitably appeal to only a fraction of the population, and will often be bored silly, as many of them are.

Of the Embassy wives who have attended our club meetings, one joined the symphony orchestra, several took horseback riding trips all through the country, one crocheted a beautiful afghan of Icelandic wools, and the last ambassador's wife really started off well by skiing "as well as a man" (an unusual mark of esteem) at the nearby skiing site. (I have only just met the new ambassador's wife and she seems quite "down to earth" and pleasant.) In general, though, the men attached to the Embassy give the impression of being diplomats in grey flannel suits with fashionable wives, and few are representative of the relaxed, unassuming and thoughtful people I used to know in America. Maybe they don't exist in this Space Age, or maybe they are not considered representative enough. The handful of natural people who do come are swiftly poured into the "diplomatic" mold and seem to lose most of their individuality.

Icelanders who are plain-spoken, eager for discussion (the men at least), and used to forming their own opinions often look askance at Americans who try to sell them democracy, when Icelanders actually practice it in more ways. They are quick to recognize sincerity, and being good listeners, quick to sense insincerity. If you wait to know them before you decide to like them, you'll never know them. You have to like them enough first to get to know them and have something of your own to offer.

* * *

This long outpouring concerning the American Embassy in Iceland is not intended as malicious criticism. It was prompted by the question of a former Embassy couple who asked, "Why is it so hard for us to get to know Icelanders?" Maybe these are some of the answers.

CHAPTER TWELVE

The World Apart

WHEN I FIRST CAME TO ICELAND, I HEARD SCATTERED REFER-
ences to the occupation days of World War II. When questioned seriously, people seemed to change the subject, feeling it was best forgotten; and I was told that after the last of
the occupying troops left, it was formally suggested that the
subject of the occupation be dropped.

Situated as the country is, southeast of Greenland and
bounded by Norway, Britain and North America, Iceland
was undoubtedly a plum for Hitler's strategic eye. Despite
the fact that by 1940 Hitler had already swallowed Austria,
Czechoslovakia, Poland, Denmark, Norway and the Nether-
lands and was soon to begin swallowing France, Iceland's
feeling of complete isolation apparently dulled her fear of

being next on the menu.

On the grey, drizzily morning of May, 1940, when Reyk-javikans awoke to find the British around them, there seems to have been more an air of stunned surprise than anything else. Iceland had never been occupied by any foreign garri-son and it took a while for rage to be succeeded by relief that it was the British, not the Germans, who invaded this little land which does not bear arms.

The British army was apparently composed of men from all walks of life. On short rations and poorly clothed, they did not look like "defenders" to Iceland. At first there were formal protests made by the government to the British Lega-tion in Reykjavik, then some whispering and a printing of notices ordering Icelandic girls not to fraternize. This must have seriously inconvenienced the enlisted men, though it seems the officers did not fare so badly. There were strains and stresses on both sides. Iceland was an unattractive and unexciting post for any soldier to defend, and though the Icelanders wished to be defended, they did not feel called upon to do much more than tolerate the defenders. But under British command, Iceland was secure and, under their supervision, Reyjavik Airport was built.

When in 1942 the British troops were needed elsewhere and neutral American troops replaced them in Iceland, the situation changed visibly. Well-dressed, well-fed and virile, the G.I.'s moved in, swelling Reykjavik's population by two-thirds. Although they looked more like "defenders" than the British troops had, most of the same strains and stresses continued between the occupying army and the Icelanders. Moreover, the Britishers, who were to leave soon, looked re-sentfully at their natty successors, and the housewives in Reykjavik were often in a dilemma.

A nice British boy came to visit one Sunday, bringing, as he always did, his weekly ration of one orange and one apple, there being no fruit at all among the Icelanders. The hostess thanked him and took the gift to the kitchen. Some minutes later a G.I. entered, bearing not a piece of fruit, but a basket of assorted fruits, and a box of chocolates to boot. Naturally the hostess was happy to receive all the fruit, but the poor British lad had deprived himself to pay his way and must not be humbled. As I remember the story, the lady solved the problem by serving the fruit to all present.

Much has been said about the morale problem during the early years of the occupation, and this problem still exists today at Keflavik, the airbase built under American supervision. Many people feel that if the British soldiers had had as many of the material conveniences as the Americans had, they would have been a good deal less miserable and better received.

During this time the Icelandic male became aware for the first time of competition from professionals at smooth talk and dating. "What can our boys expect?" one Icelandic girl explained, telling me of those bygone days. "When an Icelandic boy wants to go out with a girl, he calls her up and has her meet him inside the theatre after she has paid for her own ticket. Afterwards, he walks her home and expects to come up and spend the night with her. But when a G.I. called for a date, he arrived with flowers and transportation (the corsage for evening wear is still unknown here), helped her in and out of the car, took her to dine or dance, then thanked her for a lovely time and asked when he could see her again. He treated her like a queen!"

This, in effect, is still the most noticeable difference between Icelandic and foreign men.

I have overheard girls drinking in the honeyed line of some young soldier, apparently believing every word of it, so new does it seem. And for the soldiers, Iceland with its liberal customs is a playground—however, while the Icelandic bachelor takes care of his progeny, the soldier is not bound by obligations either moral or legal. The girls seldom realize this.

An ambiguity of feeling seems to exist between Iceland and Keflavik. Reykjavik is synonymous with Iceland, as troops and personnel at Keflavik see it; though this capital city contains almost half the population of Iceland, it is not a fair representative of Icelandic feeling toward the airbase, being actually more pro-Keflavik than other sections.

According to the Keflavik airbase viewpoint, all antagonism toward the airbase with its several thousand troops plus wives and civilians is felt by the Progressive and Communist parties, and all approval comes from the Conservative party, "who are our friends."

The Conservative party, or Independence party as it is now called, tends to be the most pro-American of the three major parties because it represents private ownership and big business. The Progressive party, representing the farmers and cooperatives, is more pro-Iceland than anything else and its attitude toward the withdrawal of troops from Keflavik seems definitely anti-American. It is almost useless to point out this difference to Americans who often find it easier to think in terms of extremes. The Social Democratic party, which is the third largest, represents white collar and some manual workers, and more or less follows the Conservative line. The Communist party, on the other hand, representing labor, is pro-Iceland, pro-Russian, and anti-American at least in theory, though I have heard that some Communists actually refuse to be seen in the company of Americans for fear it will harm their party standing.

Since 1944, coalition governments representing two or three parties have been in power. Only in the period between 1955 and 1958 has the Conservative party not been a part of the governing cabinet and once during the six congressional terms of office which have existed since Iceland achieved independence in 1944. The present government is a coalition of four Conservative and three Social Democratic cabinet ministers and is headed by Prime Minister Ólafur Thors, a picturesque gentleman of sixty-nine, whose brother Thor is Iceland's ambassador to Washington. The next parlimentary elections will be in 1962. (It is interesting to note here that the last presidential election in 1960 was insignificant compared to the excitement of U.S. presidential elections.) Iceland's president, chosen every four years, shares little in governmental duties and has much the same status as Queen Elizabeth. Now in his unopposed third term of office, President Ásgeirsson may continue as president indefinitely unless he prefers to retire. He is the second president of Iceland.

The whole matter of Communism in Iceland is extremely difficult to explain to outsiders. I can only say that in most families there is at least one member of the Communist party; and though at political or formal gatherings the men generally cluster into little political groups (as though afraid to be contaminated by fraternizing with the opposition), at family parties, of which there are many in this close family country, political differences are forgotten. It is only Americans who have been led to picture Communists as long-haired, hot-eyed individuals who carry bombs in their pockets. In truth, most Icelandic Communists are closer to

Socialists in thinking and are opposed to the idea of violence. They never discuss their politics in ordinary groups, and they keep their theories, which they may change later in life, quite separate from their day-to-day interests.

One self-styled Communist artist I knew believed that only Communists tried to practice the spirit of the Ten Commandments. He was truly idealistic and believed that there must be some other way of achieving a state of spiritual goodness than by violence. A poet's idea of Communism was to drink vodka in preference to other liquors. He always drank his vodka in the company of a bust of Stalin and the recorded music of Russian composers. Paul Robeson was one of his favorite singers, and this poet used to envision throngs of American Negroes singing not the powerful and despairing "Old Man River," but equally powerful hymns of thanks for the kind brothership of the Soviet Union. So difficult was it for the 1955 coalition government composed of Conservatives, Social Democrats and Progressives to agree on whether to appear to favor Communists, that when Halldór Laxness received the Nobel prize for literature in that year, he was not received as a cherished native son on his return to Iceland. Only a speech was made in his behalf by the Association of Icelandic Artists, but the government officials did relent by entertaining him privately the next day.

Many years ago I interviewed Mr. Laxness and he expressed surprise that my opinions did not typify the materialistic, class-conscious outlook he had associated with most Americans. I insisted that many Americans were sober, unassuming people, but I don't think he believed me at the time. Mr. Laxness was an ardent Catholic for some years, then switched to fervent communism, veered to intense socialism, and now, having published his latest book on an

Icelandic Mormon family who emigrated to Utah, he has
stated with reluctant admiration that he finds the Mormon
way of life closest to being ideal.

The number of Communists in Iceland diminished slightly
after the death of Stalin and probably more so at the time of
the Hungarian uprising of 1956. Since then the loss has been
more than recovered and now 16 to 18 per cent of the population is Communist. At about the same time as the Hungarian affair, an offshoot of the Progressive party, consisting
of leftist Progressives, joined with rightist Communists to
form the National Defense Party. Although this new group
originated from the needs of malcontents to find a platform
embodying their views, it now seems to have become merely
anti-American without being pro-anything.

There was a party of Nazi sympathizers in Iceland during
the war, which originated in Akureyri, the second largest
city in Iceland and much less cosmopolitan than Reykjavik;
and there was some goose-stepping through the streets of
Reykjavik before the coming of the British army. With the
recent upsurge of Nazi feeling in West Germany and in
America, there have been rumors of a new Nazi-Fascist
party emanating from the right-wing Conservatives, its aim
being to fight communism.

However, the emergence of this Fascist party caused less
of a ripple in the news than the very public walkout last
year of two U.S. officers from a performance of "Afternoon
of a Faun," in which the principal dancer was colored. (Since
I have mentioned this showing, which was done by the first
American ballet group to visit Iceland, I might add that
there was talk about a large number of tickets being reserved
for Keflavik servicemen for those performances. The ballets
were given in the National Theatre of Reykjavik for Ice-

landers rather than on the airbase for servicemen. Though servicemen have opportunities in America to see American ballet groups, many Icelanders who wished to attend could not get tickets.)

In regard to the recent uprisings of Negroes in the U.S., I believe most Icelanders find it a paradox to hear of race discrimination in America, which is supposed to be the cradle of liberty. Their confusion leads them to question American emissaries minutely, to the embarrassment of the latter who often are not used to such "tactlessness" and must rely strongly on their diplomacy to give impartial replies. On the other hand, Iceland has yet to face such a problem of a large-scale infiltration of a group so different in appearance from themselves (I have not heard of any Negroes in Iceland except occasional tourists or entertainers), and therefore Icelanders tend to regard the Negro problem more in a theoretical than a practical way. A year ago the newspapers announced that some members of the Icelandic government had requested that no more Negro servicemen in the NATO force be sent to Keflavik, as their presence might tend to cause friction, and that the ones already in Iceland be transferred. This request was unofficial, though word of it reached the public through the Communist party newspaper, but when the armed forces in Keflavik were reduced from roughly 3,000 to 2,000 in the spring of 1960, the mixed divisions were among those transferred.

As there have yet been no occasions for ethnic problems in Iceland, the residents still being 98 per cent Scandinavian with a common language and similar cultural traditions, so there have not arisen any religious prejudices. From time to time Jewish people have come here to reside, but having abandoned their religious differences or having ceased to practice them, they have blended quietly and pleasantly into the communities and have not formed anything so tangible as a Group, which might make the Icelanders antagonistic.

It is unfortunate that Golda Meir visited Iceland while the Eichmann trial was still in progress. She was welcomed kindly by the government, and much interest in Israeli life, especially handicrafts, was displayed by newspaper pictures and exhibitions; but the Nazi-Fascist group showed its venom at least twice. Luckily the air was cleared on both occasions before Mrs. Meir's appearance, and I doubt she heard anything of it until she left Iceland.

The Icelandic attitude about the Keflavik airbase, less noticeable now than when I first arrived, is that there is a shadow of shady dealing associated with it. The black market, which enabled many of today's wealthy Icelanders to make their start, the beginning of prostitution, the narcotics rings were all once blamed on the base. Now that the problems of prostitution and drug addiction have diminished, they are not so closely linked with Keflavik in people's minds. Opportunities for making large sums of money from the base were thwarted finally by the devaluation of the krónur in 1960, which made the legal exchange rate of the dollar almost equal to the old black-market price.

However, traces of the old antagonism about the base still exist in the feeling that a good Icelander, even a Conservative, must not be too close a buddy with the Keflavikans, that even though he may have business connections with the airfield, these connections should not include his family. Today most men prefer to drive out to the base rather than meet their associates from Keflavik in Reykjavik, where people might talk.

My early and only connection with the base was through my job as correspondent for *The Christian Science Monitor*, when I decided to investigate the "smuggling" rumors I had been hearing for some time. I laugh now at my naïveté in tackling such a crusade at a time when black-marketing was obviously a profitable business for both Americans and Icelanders. Like the detective in mediocre films who skulks in a white trenchcoat and dark glasses so you'll know he is the hero, I took the direct offensive of interviewing those in the know at Keflavik. I was treated very much as a high explosive and given elaborate assurances by a tense committee of three that there was nothing worth the slightest news interest except an occasional smuggled carton of cigarettes. (I suppose I'm not F.B.I. material at all.) I was wined and dined, driven home and presented with a free carton of cigarettes, which I politely declined for some obscure reason —call it ethics or unworldliness. Anyway, I lost my enthusiasm for crusading.

Unfavorable incidents involving Keflavik have received full publicity in all newspapers, and are nurtured lovingly by all parties during election years. About all they seem to show, however, is that there is a dearth of understanding between the two nationalities. Most of the changing will have to be made by the Americans since they are the foreigners.

From the Icelandic standpoint, it seems that the Americans on the airbase have flouted Icelandic law on some occasions, affronted Icelandic dignity and the pride of the individual, which is a strong and admirable factor here. The "love 'em and leave 'em" behavior of troops toward Icelandic women offends the national etiquette also, not so much because of what they do, but because of the cavalier and often flamboyant way in which they do it. The most deeply felt insult of all was the overnight drinking party which a group of servicemen staged with some girls on the plains of Þingvellir, the sacred seat of Iceland's earliest government. The party was as insulting to Icelanders as one staged by Khrushchev, Castro and company in the Lincoln Monument in 1960 would have been to Americans. Even the girls were chastised.

From the Keflavik viewpoint it seems that the proud, "touchy" Icelanders must be handled with kid gloves, since "the poor hicks" think they are something special.

Blood boils on both sides, as can be seen.

Coming from the atmosphere of casual plenty and assurance at Keflavik to Reykjavik is like coming from an alien land, and it is impossible to explain why I do not feel it a comedown to be married to an Icelander.

This feeling of having to take sides is confusing and disconcerting to those who wonder whether people can't be people first before being patriots. Sometimes they can, it seems, for one evening as Baldur and I sat sipping coffee in a moody little coffee cellar, an American sailor and an Icelandic boy sat down at the next table and began an eager exchange of Icelandic-English terms for the parts of a ship. I strained my ears to listen to this thoroughly natural exchange which absorbed those boys completely (more because I was interested in ships than diplomacy, I must admit). Afterwards I wondered why there must always be so much fanfare about "international relations" when they can be handled in many cases quite unobtrusively.

On the other hand, one evening when we had queued up for seats in a restaurant after a movie, an American officer in uniform settled the issue as to who would get the next table by smilingly pushing through the throng and saying in a fruity voice: "Now I know you good people won't mind

letting us sit down first," as he and his party did so. No one
spoke, of course, but I wanted to fall through the floor. I
was very careful to speak to Baldur only in Icelandic as we
waited.

During the earlier years, my interest in American uniforms
was effectually dampened by the implication that to be
accepted among solid Icelanders, I had best keep the same
distance between myself and servicemen as the Icelanders
did.

Now I see them wandering like lost sheep—scrubbed,
good boys on tour of Reykjavik, curious, well-meaning, anxious not to offend, but terribly lonely. It is then I realize the
extent of my Icelandicization, but it has gone so deep that
it often takes more courage than I possess to step forward
and be friendly and, therefore, make myself conspicuous.

Two merchant mariners, presumably from the MacCor-
mack Lines tied up at the wharf, strode into a restaurant on
Austurstraeti where I was sitting one afternoon.

A battery of eyes swept up from coffeecups and cream
cakes and searched the newcomers with unwinking stares.
After several seconds, their owners returned to the serious
business of eating. One of the sailors rubbed the back of
his neck; the other tugged up his belt.

"Nice little place, isn't it?" he ventured to his companion.
"There's a table over there."

They sat down, assembling and tucking their long legs
under the table, hitching their chairs up with a squeak.

"Well. What are we going to have?"

"Is there any meat on the menu? Is that the menu? Let's
see. Geez, if they'd only print it in English. Oh, wait a
minute!"

He stood up and strode uncertainly to the rear of the

restaurant, pausing before two doors. His hand was on one when it opened and a girl flounced out. The boy grinned weakly back at his companion, opened the other door and disappeared. He returned and slithered into his seat.

"If it says *Konur,* it's for women. If it says *Karlar* it's for us; remember that now! Brother!" They hunched over the menu.

"Look, here it says 'steak,' so help me it does. Right here —*steikt*—see? They spell it a little differently, though. Then it says *l-u-d-a*—that's how they cook it, like on French menus. Boy, could I use a steak! We've had fish for the last three days, and now that I'm on land again, I'm not going to eat anything but meat. I've almost forgotten what it tastes like. Miss," he beckoned to the waitress, "we'll have the steak."

She bent to look, smiled vaguely, nodded and went away.

From the neighboring table I watched them, amused at first and then concerned. Was it any of my business to interfere? I was an American; I could help them, but was it any of my business? Then it came over me that I was doing just what the Icelanders do—minding my own business because no one asked me for help. Also, prudishly, I was a married woman and they were servicemen. But I was American! Or was I? Unable to watch any longer, I beat a cowardly retreat before the waitress could come with two plates of fried flounder. She too had known that *steikt* isn't steak, but she also was too shy to explain.

The flavor of Reykjavik has noticeably changed since the war years and has become distinctly American. This may partly explain the Icelanders' reluctance to court "little America," as the base is often called, when many feel its influence is already great enough. Though there has been a steady increase in the use of English in the past five years,

Danish still remains the first foreign language taught in the schools, Denmark still remains the Paris of the north for Icelanders, the trend in furniture is Scandinavian modern, and women's fashions are not the casual American styles, but the chic and elegant European ones.

Despite all the problems created by the presence of foreign armies, Iceland has had little alternative but to accept some form of military personnel. After the war, according to previous agreement with the United States, the American troops in Iceland were evacuated by the end of 1947. However, Keflavik airport still remained under the supervision of several successive American contracting companies which, according to agreement, were to train young Icelanders to gradually replace American personnel and to keep the airfield open and operating. Perhaps the least friction occurred during those years from 1947 to 1951, for there were few aircraft workers compared to the 65,000 (45,000 of which were American) Allied troops in Iceland during the war; furthermore, the workers were civilians. In 1949 Iceland became a member of the North Atlantic Pact but refused to grant peacetime bases in Iceland to any foreign power. Following the Korean War, however, Iceland changed her mind, and in 1951 agreed to have American troops stationed at Keflavik. Again uniforms were visible, though far fewer than before, and again the frictions arose. Though these troops were and are still here as part of the NATO forces, the focus of antagonism remains unchanged.

In the summer of 1960 some Icelanders staged a peaceful demonstration by walking the thirty-five miles from Keflavik to Reykjavik. Although this began as a pro-Iceland action to make the country realize that the threat of war was not so imminent as when the troops were last asked to stay on in 1956, it was turned into or construed to be a Communist, anti-American demonstration. The idea has often been expressed, however, that if the airbase were turned over entirely to Iceland, rather than being under the aegis of NATO but run by the Americans, then Iceland could resign its NATO membership and be as neutral as Switzerland.

The Communists are naturally against NATO. The attitude of other Icelanders is influenced by two factors: Iceland has never engaged in war and she does not wish to; but because she is a NATO member and because of the base at Keflavik, she might be drawn into the midst of an international war, though she had only given economic support to NATO.

In addition to these points, it must be remembered that despite the amiable feeling Iceland really has for the United States, the cold fact remains that Iceland is very dependent economically on other nations for most of her raw materials and much of her food. Whether her trade swings primarily to East or West will be more a matter of economics than political ideology.

It seems many people would rather be poorer, more peaceful and less progressive without the Keflavik base.

CHAPTER THIRTEEN

Don't Kick Mamma, Darling!

CHILDREN ARE VERY DEFINITELY HERE TO STAY IN ICELAND. MORE are born here proportionately than in western Europe and the United States, and the infant mortality rate is half that of the U.S.

In the resident Wives' Club, most of the women have three or four children—it is a rare season when someone is not expecting. The women from the American Embassy who most often come to our club meetings are those who have the most children; and women without children say they have never felt their childlessness so keenly as in Iceland.

Among married women, children and fashions are the most popular topics for conversation. Married men too talk of their children, but are more naturally interested in their offsprings' achievements than in their care and upbringing, which falls almost entirely in the mothers' hands.

My life with children could be a book in itself, and I can only wonder whether other mothers have any more privacy than I have. At times children seem to crawl out of the woodwork. It must be my fault, for since they were very young, I have encouraged such creative pastimes as crayons and watercolors, clay modeling and scrapbook making, rather than heaving them out of the house as is usually done here.

In what I consider bad weather, I don't have the heart to refuse to let other woeful little souls come in, though their mothers have told them to stay outdoors because the fresh air is good for them. Moreover, Icelandic women usually succeed in confining their children to one room for activities, whereas I fight a losing battle against confusion in every room. When other women clean house, they send their children out. And "out" to the children often means our house. My housecleaning is done in spite of children, but poor Baldur seldom sees results, for by the time he comes home, the house looks exactly as it did when he left. And so do I.

As I say, my house is not as clean as my neighbors', but when I have a few moments to reflect, I think my way has much to commend it. So far, at least, I know who my children's playmates are, something of what they talk about, and even more of their play methods, manners, intelligence and creative ability. However, I do not like strange children wandering through my bedroom, looking through the drawers along with my hospitable sons, standing hungrily at the doorframe while we dine, and making themselves at home in the livingroom with comic books when they haven't even greeted me or answered my greeting. Nor do I appreciate their imperious ringing of the doorbell at half-second intervals, barely five minutes after I've just sent out my brood, to ask me exactly where each child is. The three-year-olds who seem to visit only so they can try out our bathroom are more friendly, however; they often outtalk me, but again I resent having to get them back into their five layers of clothing plus mittens and boots as the reward for being their unsuspecting hostess. And I still feel mean and resentful when I bring home a treat of four apples, four licorice sticks, or something else divided equally for peace, to discover that there is a "guest" who is hungry. Sometimes, to avoid this dilemma, I buy two extra treats "for Mamma and Pabbi," and if there are no little strangers, we actually get to eat them ourselves.

Sometimes I wonder whether it is I who am crazy or the children. They do not infringe on Baldur's privacy—maybe he's too ordinary—but let Mamma retreat to the bathroom, and there are frantic pleas from everyone to be let in. (As I write this, I notice that the carbon to page 86 is being folded into an airplane. Excuse while I shake the daylights out of Jakie.) If I lock the front door to take a bath in the daytime—I have to grab my chances—one of two things happens: Either they all stream out, coatless, leaving the door open and leaving me to answer the doorbell or telephone which invariably ring; or, feeling lonely, they open the lock on the bathroom door with a screwdriver or scissors and come in to watch and make bright conversation. I find it a grueling ordeal in this house where I am the only female. One day as I stepped into my underthings, I butted one child under the chin with one knee and kicked the other child, who was standing behind me, in the stomach with the other foot.

"Ye gods," I shrieked while they howled, "can't I even

put on a pair of pants in peace?"

And do some people really have boudoirs? My adorning is done amidst a battery of critical eyes and free advice.

Once, while making up for a party, I had neglected to put a padlock on the bedroom door—this was at a country inn. The seven-year-old son of the owner sauntered in, leaned his elbows on the table and began to shift his eyes back and forth from mirror to me. Finally he ventured to ask:

"Are you putting that stuff on your face so you'll be beautiful?"

"Yes," I said flatly. After several moments of wry anticipation, I even managed a brave smile.

Later, in the dining hall, surrounded by about a dozen men, my little pal interrupted the conversation to ask in his sweet, childish voice, "Why do you have such a big nose?"

"Why do you have such a little one?" I countered and saved the day, for he began to finger his own little tip-tilt in astonishment. Alas, victories over children are never triumphant endings, only minor points in an eternal skirmish.

I feel that Icelandic parents often take the easiest way out with their children and let them have what they want just to avoid arguments, whereas most of the time I have to sift and weigh the request and practice psychology. I don't know which is the better method, but most Icelandic mothers seem to find four children less harassing than I do.

Yet when I have been reduced to frustrated incoherence by a rainy day with them, my three-year-old will volunteer, "I go to the store for you, Mamma," and he will, though it takes him an hour to travel the four blocks. My four-year-old will announce, "I'm going to pick up all the toys in my room," and does it. My eight-year-old will quietly grab a broom and sweep the entire house clean, or he will paint especially for

me a picture of a sun squeezing happily out from between
two mountains. And my eldest will say, "Mamma, isn't it
nice that God made birds to fly? If they just sat on the
ground we'd have to be close to hear them, but since they
can fly, there is singing all through the air. Isn't it nice?"
And it is.

Icelandic mothers feed their children fully and frequently
from the time they are pint size. During the early months a
visiting nurse comes regularly to weigh and check the diet
of the baby. Though this is supposed to be a convenience,
it always seemed to me that she managed to call just after
I had the baby swathed to the nose and put out to sleep.
By the time I had awakened him and unclothed him, to be
weighed, I would be in a rather unreceptive mood.

Every time the nurses came, they added a new item to the
diet. (I secretly followed Dr. Benjamin Spock, whose book
was somehow obtained by every American wife as soon as
she had her baby in Iceland and consulted as a Bible. Spock
is so comforting. Even if your baby has two heads, Spock
manages to make you feel that it is by no means an unusual
phenomenon, though perhaps not common, and that the
mother should not torture herself with apprehensions, but
should let the pediatrician see the child.) From the records
of my last baby, I see that vitamins and formula were pre-
scribed for the first month, orange juice (whether available
or not) the next week, then skýr, cereal and carrots, potatoes, rutabagas and egg yolk by the time the baby was
two and a half months old. I struggled with formulas and
sterilizing forever, it seems, though Icelandic women I knew
owned only one or two bottles which they would casually
prepare for the feedings and let the baby finish sometime
later whenever he let out a squawk. Their babies developed

no more sicknesses than mine did and were probably a lot more placid as a result of this offhand treatment.

The visiting nurse often censured me for not being regular with the orange juice feedings. With everything else to do, I often forgot it for several days at a time.

"Mix it with his milk," she suggested.

"It curdles the milk."

"It will curdle in his stomach anyway," she returned, "just mix it."

I did and the curds wouldn't go through the nipple, so I relapsed into my sinful ways.

My one-and-only has winged, pixie-like ears which, added to his upturned nose and slanted eyes, give him an elfin look. (He won't like reading this.) The eyes and nose are fine, and so are the ears—I give you Clark Gable. But what of one ear? My third son, Eiríkur, had one ear poised for flight and the other folded close to his sweet little head. Baldur insisted that the prominent ear had character, but I was one for consistency. I taped down the offending one, and each time the tape was removed by the nurse, who thought it silly to try to change nature.

"But how could such a thing have happened?" I inquired.

"Obviously he inherited one ear from you and the other from your husband," she explained. I guess that was it. I must say it gives Eiríkur a certain joyous alert appearance unlike that of my others.

The visiting nurses were kind, though, and it was nice to have the babies weighed at home. Between the nurses and Spock, my babies all gained well, but were never fat. I'm sure my neighbors thought I didn't feed them enough. As a matter of fact, when I first arrived in Iceland with my 115 pounds of sylphdom, it was commented that Americans were rich but they certainly were undernourished. Now that I have attained 120 pounds of rounded shoulders, mushy midriff and corded biceps, no one bothers to comment, for it's the fashion to be slender. The youngsters coming up now certainly seem to be narrower and finer-boned than their elders. Is it diet or the quickened pace of living that has changed the body structure? Anyway, Icelandic babies are quite robust-looking, seldom delicate or fragile in appearance, even in facial structure. Since they are fed constantly from the bottle stage up, it is not surprising that few of them are thin.

It is a fact that little children here need a good layer of fat to help them withstand the weather, which they are exposed to at an early age. Many times I have passed a parked baby carriage shrouded with an adult raincoat, which I had thought quite empty, only to find that beneath the raincoat, carriage covers, eiderdown, several sweaters and hats is a soundly sleeping tot.

Toddlers are equipped with minute rubber boots and warm sweaters and leggings, and play for long hours outside. The mother seldom has to watch them too carefully, for she is besieged with offers from eager six- to ten-year-olds to tend the babies outside. Usually, any children nearby automatically keep an eye on the small ones. This is a great blessing because there are few sidewalks yet, most of them are graveled and have no curbs, and Reykjavik children generally play on the streets. Participants in hopscotch, jumprope, ball games, and the tricycle traffic all scatter to the sides when cars come. It helps to have an older child shout that a truck is approaching and shepherd the little ones to safety. Also the rule forbidding unnecessary horn blowing makes an oncoming car even more dangerous. Unless you have good ears, or the wind is blowing with you, an uneasy feeling may cause you to turn around only to see a car silently tracking you two yards away. I am all for night silence, but I do think autos ought to toot briskly in the daytime. But the big children watch the little ones, and the little ones are known to the neighborhood. My first proud moment of motherhood came when on the street one little acorn said to another, "That's *Tryggvi's* Mamma!"

In Reykjavik, ages three to six can attend nursery schools run by the private Child-Care Association for half or a full day at a worthwhile cost to the parent (consequently, there is a long waiting list). Here the children spend much of their time outside in the play yard, where there may be a discarded dory or an old automobile chassis for their special delight when they are discontented with regular equipment. Inside, they learn a variety of folk songs, color, paint, work with clay and hear stories. Each child takes with him his afternoon "coffee" of a coke bottle of milk and a sweet bun.

Children begin first grade when they are seven, though they may have learned to read the year before in a private school. When his child starts first grade, the foreign parent often feels a first pang of helplessness at having to coach him in homework. Willing and able to do the three R's, the parent discovers that arithmetic exercises have different symbols, are laid out and calculated differently, so that even though he can find the right answer by his own method, he must follow the teacher's method. (Schools are crowded and hours so short—three hours daily—that only the theory and rudiments can be taught in school; practice must be gained at home.) The Icelandic style of penmanship with its ornate curlicues and flourishes—beautiful to see, but a real hindrance to rapid writing—must be practiced as taught in the school. A mother has little chance of helping her child to read when her accent is poor and the phonetic system is not used.

I marvel at the children who nevertheless learn to read though they have not been taught to sound out a word, only spell it by letters. All my boys have been slow readers at first because of the double-language problem. This frustrates them and discourages me, but the teachers assure us that their second tongue will be a real asset when they begin to study foreign languages when they are twelve. A foreign parent can seldom help his child study history, geography and poetry, when he must first study those subjects himself. I feel keenly disappointed that I cannot dip into my remembrance of history, etc., to enlighten or amuse the children in a helpful way. The explorers and statesmen, the warriors and wars of America will be little more than names to them till they reach university level. Of the scores of songs I know, only a few are Icelandic. Baldur knows but few of mine, and though the children sometimes take a fancy to one tune or another, they would rather sing what all their friends sing.

This is indeed a helpless time in other ways, for by a certain age, usually when they are seven or eight years old, the children have a horror of seeming different. Mother must speak in Icelandic and behave exactly as other mothers do so their friends won't "hee on them" (a remarkably descriptive phrase meaning to snicker at someone). My normal impulse is to greet little visitors and engage them in some conversation. Now my boys tell me that other mothers ignore the visitors and do not question them, and the boys feel acutely embarrassed if I do otherwise.

Then there is always the question as to when to speak Icelandic with children when English might have a better

effect. I reprove my children in English to save their feelings, but otherwise speak Icelandic when they are with
friends. I used to scold their friends in Icelandic, but they
would double up with laughter at my grammar; now I scold
in a torrent of English, and they understand the import if
not the words. My greatest frustration comes in trying to
explain in Icelandic to a group of children why it's better
to tackle each other's legs than punch in the head or torso,
why when throwing snowballs, it's easier (and safer) to aim
at the body (which is padded with clothes) than the face,
and why nooses must be put under the armpits rather than
around the neck when playing "horse."

I seem to be overconscientious about play rules, however.
When my children damage someone's toy, and the weeping
owner comes to my door, I mete out lectures and/or punishment, but have heard other mothers say that they never
interfere with the children's fights. They will become angry
and take measures only if a coat is badly torn (which the
mother has to repair), or a window broken (which the
father has to pay for). So far as I have seen, there is no code
of fair play instilled by parents. The children eventually
develop it themselves or, rather, stand alone and fight their
battles. Whereas one boy might stone five separate boys as
they pass by him, those five victims would not think of gang-
ing up on the stone-thrower. And they would rather avoid
him later than take revenge. Even at this age, they don't act
as a group, and perhaps that is why there are fewer and
less vicious fights than in other countries.

After the age of three, and until high school, a boy would
be caught dead rather than wear a red jacket, pink pajamas
or a raincoat other than black. For some reason these are
sissy colors, though they may wear red shirts or sweaters.

Here, the drabbest, darkest colors are considered "manly" by little boys, and all the bright colors which would give a lift to the spirits and enable parents and motorists to spot children from afar are considered suitable only for girls and babies. It is a pity, but so the custom goes.

A boy may own shoes, but if all his pals clump around in boots outside and pad around the house in thick, woolen socks, out go the shoes except on special occasions when he will announce to pedestrians, "I am elegant today." If one boy sees another in shoes with hair brushed on a weekday, the immediate question is, "Why are you so elegant today?" And the answer to this unsarcastic question is, proudly, "I'm going visiting, or to a party." Then the elegant one may swagger a bit, and the booted one will fidget in his boots and scamper off to join other unelegant companions.

From age ten to thirteen, children are busy most of the time with school and its staggered hours, plus compulsory extra subjects such as swimming, gymnastics, sewing and carpentry. It's a hectic pace for their legs and stomachs, because meals are snatched at odd hours to the woe of mothers with several school children, and the distances they walk are often great. But I've stopped pitying them; all the children have those crazy schedules and never feel sorry for themselves.

Last spring Tryggvi, who was nine and in third grade, had some three hours of daily instruction (including Saturday) from noon to three o'clock. To the daily thirty-five-minute sessions of reading (which included folk tales, short essays on history, geography and natural history), writing, and arithmetic, were added two weekly classes of spelling and one in poetry. Wednesdays and Fridays he raced home to gulp a glass of milk and ran back for gym at 3:45, to return

with dripping hair from the compulsory after-gym shower.
(I must say that he showed more enthusiasm for these show-
ers than for baths at home. I understand that most eight-
and nine-year-olds feel it sissyish to be overclean.) Thursday
mornings at 9:00 A.M. there were carpentry classes, lasting
two hours, and held in another school a mile away. Last year
also, he joined the Cub Scouts, but his enthusiasm dulled
quickly, for after trudging to this distant school for Sunday
morning meetings in the dark winter, he found that the
activities usually consisted of a rambling walk through the
suburbs, and a further chilling and tiring walk back home in
time for dinner.

Before last year, Rikki, who is a year younger, began his
schooldays at 10:00 A.M. Thus Tryggvi ate at 11:45, Baldur,
I and the younger children had our noon meal at 12:30, and
Rikki at 1:15. It was usually two o'clock before the kitchen
was clear, coffeetime or snacktime was from three to four,
and supper preparations began at six. Last spring's schedule,
enabling both boys to attend school after noon, seemed no
trouble at all by contrast, but I pity the mothers who have
three or more children in different grades at different hours
and are inevitably in the house all day serving food. Most
laborers take a lunch with them, but office workers like
Baldur usually come home for the noon meal and expect
a hearty, hot one.

I have learned to my surprise that in elementary and junior
high schools, girls rather than boys present a disciplinary
problem. For punishment, recalcitrant lads may be shifted
to the girls' section, but the reverse treatment would be welcomed by the girls. Since Icelanders don't believe in spanking or harming others physically, especially women, the
girls learn early to take advantage of this. "In the old days

when Mamma was young and Jesus lived a few streets away," as my boys used to construe it, it was the boys who were the problem. A girl's pride could be sufficiently hurt by making her sit in a corner with or without a dunce cap, refusing her permission to go out for recess, or inviting her to stay an hour after school, during which time she would write fifty times on blackboard or paper "*I will not whisper in class.*" Fifty lines of this can give you a pain in the arm, as I well know.

Because children react in different ways to punishment, it is always a complex problem to find suitable punishments or to decide whether to punish at all. I have observed that Icelanders tend to ignore many small mistakes and punish their children only for the important ones; hence the children learn to differentiate between misdemeanors and illegal behavior. It also saves the children from being constantly nagged.

I find it difficult to compromise between the rights of children and the rights of parents, but because of the national indulgence toward children, I probably give in to mine more often than I might in America. Nevertheless, I am insistent on honesty. After one dreadful scene which all my boys remember and I shall never forget, we have achieved "honesty." As it happened, one of them had committed a last-straw wrongdoing and wouldn't own up. Everyone was innocent, but one was guilty; and even with my instinct for knowing what each might do, a little psychology, and the "eyes in the back of my head," I couldn't figure out which boy was the culprit. With horrible misgivings, I very firmly ordered them all outdoors until one confessed. It was raining and they all cried, some were hurt, and one was defiant. Even the baby insisted on joining them rather than staying with his irate mother, though I knew that he at least was not guilty. They sobbed outside while I experienced agonies of guilt, but I felt I had to see the issue through. After fifteen minutes, I let them in and ordered them to their rooms, where for a half hour they continued their hysterics. I had twisted their personalities forever, I thought, as I tried to calm myself in the kitchen. Finally I had the sense to pose a leading question to the most defiant one, and he unwittingly confessed. I apologized with tears to each of the others for not having believed them. The guilty one was also hugged, for the memory of the punishment his brothers had shared was enough censure. That night we had a long talk, Baldur included, and resolved that from that day on wrongdoers if questioned were to confess immediately, whether they would be punished or not, for a family can't hang together without honesty.

Now the confessions come quickly, and take the edge off my anger before it's had time to build up, and I am far more careful about punishing. I can look anyone proudly in the eye when they accuse one of my children of a wrong. If he has denied it, I believe him, and it's a thrilling feeling. And if my children as adults are secretly nervous at being dishonest, I think it is a good thing, even in this age where honesty has only a relative meaning.

CHAPTER FOURTEEN

Come of Age!

ALL OF A SUDDEN WE GROW UP. FOR YEARS WE HAVE BEEN carefree and uninhibited, taking our parents' words as golden truths, relying on them automatically when we need guidance, coming home tired from play to fall into uncomplicated sleep. We do our lessons by rote in school and are the bullies or the bullied, depending on our temperament, and boys are noisy, uncombed creatures who win all our marbles from us, feel ashamed if we can high-jump better than they, and thankfully keep to themselves. Then suddenly things change. Overnight, it seems, we become aware of ourselves as individuals, and the innocent days are over. We are furtive and shy instead of straightforward. We see that our parents sometimes contradict themselves and are not omniscient after all. Our studies assume new dimensions, and we thrill to phrases we have been immune to before. Life sparkles all around us and beckons to us no matter what we do.

We stare into our mirrors, and are surprised that our faces seem the same, for suddenly our whole secure world is gone, and we are at the beginning of a new one, timorous, unprepared and painfully vulnerable. Respected elders are now objects of scorn. The foods we liked, the clothes we liked, no longer appeal—we do not even like ourselves any more. We try to rush back, fasten on roller skates again, for the last time, and are humiliated by a barked knee when we fall. We sneak outdoors to roll down a grassy slope as we did only a week ago in wild enjoyment; we get up, brushing off the grass, and feel a little foolish. Night no longer means bedtime, it means sitting outside watching twilight fall and the stars come out, while we sit filled with a nameless, almost overpowering yearning for something.

Nobody understands us. Everyone is against us. We are often silent now with our girl friends instead of chattering uninterruptedly, and we are not so close as before, both realizing this and not knowing why. The dirty, uncombed boys are clean now and do not meet our glances any more than we meet theirs. Most horrible of all, we blush. Our parents talk together about us behind closed doors, and we realize we are no longer children, but soon to become *women*—oh, the frightening fecundity of that word! We will *not* grow up, we decide defiantly, and tease our young brother and put on childish dress to conceal our developing figures, and throw snowballs at each other.

And all the time we know there is no going back. We look rather desperately to the future and are violent in our hates and loves, vicious in our criticisms, passionate in our sorrow.

We are formless units of compressed energy, sprouting feelers on all sides, unable to hold ourselves back, yet ineffectual in our strivings. A whole new world of delights and dangers has opened to us and we are not prepared. What is wisdom? How can you learn it! They call us adolescents, and they smile in their smugness and say, "You'll outgrow it." How can *they* know? How can they *know!*

Many years later we become parents. We have forgotten our young selves, and the sight and signs of that awakening in our children make them incomprehensible to us; we fear for them and are aware of our helplessness. We could help, we want to help, but we are all fumbles and stammers. Besides, they are turning away already because we sound stuffy and bossy. When, if ever, will they turn back to us as people, not children, and let us help a little? We are not omniscient —don't blame us—and we never were. *We're* still learning to be *parents.* We have to be against you sometimes *for your own good.*

* * *

So at twelve or thirteen, depending on his birthdate, the Icelandic youngster is confirmed, and after that comes the beginning of big problems, for at confirmation age theoretically he becomes an adult. Now comes a noticeable increase of freedom for him. True to the policy of non-interference, the parents relinquish their concern for the welfare of their child's soul—if it has ever concerned them up to this point. Because parents here consider their duty to their children to be confined to feeding and clothing them, they are often unequipped to deal with the many-faceted individual who emerges during adolescence after they have pushed him outdoors. The parents' solution to the problem is to push the child out again and, when he does come home, they confine him to his room where he may bring his friend or friends. The parents never peek. What the teenager does is his own business! Being Icelandic, he will not offer to account for his time and the parents, respecting another's privacy, will not question. The mother's excuse is that she is endlessly busy with her housekeeping, and the father is busy with his job, resting, listening to the radio or reading.

When questions about sex are asked, most Icelandic mothers seem to feel that the less said, the better. "Send them to the farm in the summers; it's so good for them at this age," they often say. For there, among other things, they will have ample opportunity to watch the animals mating, and then there will be no need for explanations.

This casual way of looking at sexual maturity makes us foreign wives apprehensive, for we still feel that love and sex should go together. But there are no such niceties or compunctions here. One's intimacies are of no concern to anyone else, parents included, no matter what one's age might be. A fast reputation is bad only in the sense that when the person marries he might find it more difficult to remain faithful than one who has only had a few affairs. A baby born out of wedlock is endured as a necessary evil of the moral system. Even though a girl's reputation is unblemished by an illegitimate baby, she is apt to be more cautious about getting involved the next time.

I know from conversations that a small baby given to the grandparents for upbringing is an accepted but irritating responsibility for them. They feel it unfair, and justly so. Yet more closeness between parents and child might make less likely the flippant rejoinder made by one young girl about making her baby legitimate and marrying its father:

"No, I don't want to marry him. He's a jerk. I never even liked him."

Luckily, the illegitimate child bears no stigma himself. It is difficult enough to have only one parent while his friends have two; because he has only a mother, his standard of living will undoubtedly be lower.

Many times I have heard foreign women say: "I wish I could send my children away for their adolescence. I don't want them to grow up as morally lax as the children are here"; or "How can we protect our daughters when the life they move in contradicts our teachings?"; or "Why are they so brazen? There's a ten-year-old girl who keeps phoning my fourteen-year-old boy at night, and he's not interested in girls yet. Why doesn't she leave him alone?"

Because Icelandic youngsters do not date, there are no standards for dating or "going steady." In separate groups they walk on the streets, go to dances or on trips. And if they get together after the street patrol or dance or during the trip, who is to know or tell? And who would question? Sex knowledge is one thing you can't ignore and hope will go away. What happens is that the youngster has to learn for himself. It is short-sighted of parents to expect that teen-agers will act maturely when they do not yet know how.

The oversimplified situation is this: that too much is given and too little returned. The running of the house is the woman's job, and the wage-earning the man's. The wife is not expected to help her man in his job (farming couples excepted), nor is he expected to help in the house. The children demand and their demands are fulfilled whenever possible, for all is done to keep them from the hardships that have helped to build the characters of their parents. When the children take jobs, it is for clothes and pocket money, thus helping in an indirect way, but they are seldom encouraged or obliged to contribute to the home. If they do not have jobs, they still feel little obligation to help, since, traditionally, the mother runs the home.

As in continental Europe, the boy is preparing for a craft, or business or a professional career, and the girl is anticipating housekeeping and motherhood. It is true that each sex knows where it is going, and is spared the very real anxieties of career competition suffered by American teenagers, but there is little to bring them together as friends. Higher education is available for girls, but though they are free to study indefinitely, few do, believing it a possible hindrance to marriage.

Because their interests are so separated by tradition, there are few activities for both boys and girls. There are plenty of political and community houses, but there are no supervised youth clubhouses, where teenagers can bowl, play table tennis or cards, hold informal discussions, or even dance to jukeboxes. If they want to dance, they must go to a public place with an orchestra, and though they can order only soft drinks until they are eighteen, someone always has a bottle out in the car or in a pocket. There are bus trips to the country for pleasure, but few hiking or bicycling trips.

At present there are two large sports stadiums in Reykjavik: one connected with the University and built by private sportclub funds, which seats about 10,000 people; the other built by the government seats about 14,000 spectators of soccer and occasional track or wrestling events. Because of the weather, both these stadiums are used only during the summer months and are not used for circuses, horse racing, or mass celebrations. A few years ago, an American skating enthusiast tried to push the idea of having freezing pipes installed beneath the University stadium grounds to permit winter-long ice skating, but the idea was not used. For one thing, the private sport clubs and the government, which would pay for the installation, were probably not interested in ice skating themselves. It is rare to see any adult over twenty-one, except for an athlete, skating. This is not yet considered fashionable exercise for adults. If it were possible to convert parts of these stadiums for ice skating or roller skating, it would not only increase their usage, but would also provide young people with two participant sports which both sexes could enjoy.

Parents do not encourage supervised teenage parties in the home and therefore, they have little opportunity to know their children's friends or the friends' parents. They always try to avoid interfering. The assumption is that they don't care about their children. But they *do*. It was different in the country, where families knew those on neighboring farms, where one farmer helped out another with his haymaking or sheep gathering, and the young people were always around and knew each other. In Reykjavik, though, there are no such opportunities, and everyone is a stranger. The livingroom is a sacred place, which must always be orderly, but surely a fortnightly session of scuffed floors and sandwiches, with definite rules for smoking, drinking and general behavior, regular sessions of games and chatter and dancing should be a welcome alternative to having youngsters go out among strangers every time. A house party encourages a comparing of interests, whereas there is little time or quiet at a dance for anything but flirtations.

Because of this restricted situation, the strongest bond between boy and girl is naturally a very basic one. Thence comes the phenomenon, strange even to my American eyes, of the female blatantly pursuing the preoccupied or seemingly reluctant male. Except during courtship, men never phone girls; they tell the girls to call *them*. It is demeaning for a man to seem to solicit a girl's attention. Such a reversal of roles is not due to a shortage of men but to the fact that the girls feel there is nothing else of interest to do.

Yet no matter how strongly we criticize and resent the moral liberties in Iceland, we Americans, perhaps more than other foreign groups, must finally examine our own confusing moral system and decide whether that is better.

Coming from a country where sex standards are by tradition different for men and women to one where such standards do not prevail, we cannot say to our sons: "Sow your wild oats discretely with 'experienced girls' (who give what they promise), and then marry a girl who is chaste (if there are any left after said advice)"; or to a daughter, "Don't sleep with anyone until you marry. (Naturally, however, don't be frigid or disinterested. Learn to promise and refuse in the same breath for love is romance, but sex is sin.)" We cannot say these things, for we are not bringing up our children in America. What we can say is, "Try to be as selective in love as in other things. Spend your affections wisely; don't short-change yourself."

If it is childbirth out of wedlock to which we object, I believe we are justified in saying sternly to a daughter: "We parents are not going to raise your offspring. Our raising days are over; we have done our duty. And if you become an unwed mother, your days of freedom will be over for a long time, and your clothes money will go for diapers." To a son we should say, "A child out of wedlock can cost you a lot of money for a long time, slow up your career preparations, and cause future problems with the girl you eventually marry."

If it is the promiscuity we are against, as is more likely, perhaps we can say, "If your pleasures and interests are only sexual, you will never develop the capacity to appreciate anything deeper. Wait till you find someone who shares your interests and your outlook on life, and then give your heart as well as your body."

What can we tell these teenagers that will give them time to grow to adulthood without having it thrust upon them too soon? I suppose they will find their answers in their own ways, as people do; and we parents can only hope and pray, as all parents do, and as our own did.

CHAPTER FIFTEEN

Who's That Knocking at My Door?

BEFORE I CAME HERE, I CONSIDERED MYSELF AN EASYGOING person with normal emotions and a good imagination which I ascribed to a spark of brilliance—the kind that remains hidden whenever it's supposed to show itself. Since I've been in Iceland, however, I seem to express my emotions in italics. I am as easygoing as a chess player. I get spring fever in January and am depressed enough in June to buy a boat ticket anywhere. What I had thought was an imagination is practically astral projection. The jet of brilliance has, disappointingly, remained in abeyance except in such instances as when my number two son asks, "Mamma, why can't we have a rabbit?" and I reply, "Too much competition." Thank you, Mrs. Líndal.

It's disconcerting to find that no one here scoffs at prophetic dreams or ghost stories. Even astrology is tolerated. Mediums and other possessors of extrasensory perception are no rarity, and their revelations have often been so startling that if people laugh at them, it is often with a feeling of uneasiness. There are of course plenty of fakes, but there are some mediums who should not be judged harshly too quickly.

I have seen no ghosts in the dining room, though my eldest once claimed he did. Nor did I see the lady in white who passed through our bedroom one night, though Baldur insists he was awake at the time. But I have seen a message appear on a Ouija board and come true so vividly that the lady whom the message concerned will not play again. And when a housewife-cardreader told me of a "bad news" letter in the post, followed by a very "good news" letter, my curiosity was really aroused. On my return home that Saturday afternoon, there was no letter but "in the post" means "on the way," I assured myself. On Monday, a regular day for mail from the U.S., I received a letter saying that my ninety-one-year-old grandmother had gone into the hospital with a sudden inexplicable sickness. And on Tuesday, a day on which home mail seldom arrives, there were two letters. One from my agent in New York telling me that the publishers were still interested in my book and wondered whether there was any fresh news of it. The second letter was a gratifyingly enthusiastic one from my sister who had just received and read all rough installments of the book. These were really "good news" letters after a tiring and depressing winter. The fortuneteller had mentioned in connection with the "bad news" letter that it did not contain death news, and that she saw an elderly, sick person who would shortly recover. A couple of weeks later, I learned that my grandmother's illness had subsided by itself and was probably only a symptom of old age. Since that important Saturday I have visited this same clairvoyant frequently and regard her prophecies with great respect.

Iceland can rouse the imagination of the dullest, and I'm the sort who doesn't cringe when reading murder mysteries at night—I merely get up several times to *make sure* I locked the door.

Wind in the darkness in America meant being snug inside, or at least the neighborly sound of traffic and lights of houses if one had to be outdoors. Here I stumble down a rutted road on a pitchy night with neither moon nor streetlights, and the sound of the wind in the telephone wires making my flesh crawl; and when another pedestrian staggers into sight, I look to see whether he casts a shadow before I feel at ease, or at least I make sure the stagger is due to wind and road.

One night in a snowstorm, I alighted from a bus on a lonely road, somewhere on which a fellow American lived. After the bus moved away, I got the full play of the wind, plus the crashing obbligato of ocean waves from the nothingness on the far side of the road. It had snowed heavily for some days and, as I stepped back to check my directions, I tumbled head first into a snowdrift. Talk of being buried alive. You never saw such a scrabbling of hands and feet before I finally emerged, gasping and weak with fright.

The southeast wind is terrific in the suburbs where we live. Occasionally it reaches hurricane force and the weather bureau calls it "foul weather." On one such day, Eiríkur, then four years old, went out in the wind, got as far as the mesh fence next door, and clung there, crying miserably as the "pimples" (hail) beat on his face. The fence top was five feet from the ground and he was on the other side. How one's children make one brave! I rushed out, was blown swiftly to the fence, jumped so that my stomach balanced on the top, leaned, hoisted his forty pounds up and over against the wind, jumped down in a half turn and was back in the house before I remembered that wind terrifies me.

Another such day when the school children were being blown across the street as they left school (the school finally ordered a bus to deliver them home safely), I had visions of my nine-year-old struggling home alone against the elements—five long blocks in the teeth of the wind and high on a hill. Really gritting my teeth, I warned the others to stay inside and set out in the yellow-grey world to meet Tryggvi. My coat was like a sail as I ran most of the way to the deserted school, to be told that all the children had left. Aghast at the vision of him shivering in a ditch along the way, I retraced my steps. For every three mad strides forward, a gust would sweep me two steps back. Halfway home a terrific thrust blew me to my knees. Bowing before the elements, I got up, courageous as a jellyfish, and clung to an auto chassis nearby, wondering how I'd ever get home and where my son was. Fortunately, a jeep came along and, though as an adopted Icelander I rarely ask for help, I flagged it down and climbed in before the driver could speak and directed him to turn around and take me straight home. Some minutes later I arrived and stumbled up the steps into the house. Tryggvi greeted me nonchalantly.

"Why did the man drive you home?" he asked.

"I couldn't walk. The wind was so strong. How did you

get here," I babbled, still weak.

"I took a short cut from school down to our street and just walked. It was fun."

I suspect he added the last part with bravado, but whenever the wind blows strong from the southeast, I still break out in a cold sweat, my heart starts thudding, and squeamishly, I put Eiríkur out to test his equilibrium before I trust myself to go buy milk. Now I've learned to run against the wind and to crawl if necessary.

No one can say my imagination has stagnated. Some years ago we climbed Hverfjall in the north of Iceland. Actually it's only a rim of a mountain, for the center was blown out completely by an eruption some hundreds of years ago. The inside of the crater resembles a deserted football stadium with a small bandstand in the center. While Baldur and his father collected stones of geological interest, I sang at the top of my lungs, and found the acoustics perfect in that windless, walled crater. Finally we started back, climbing up the inner wall. Coming up over the ridge an hour before, I had pitied Baldur's old father, who walked far behind us with a cane and refused all aid. But now, on the way back, his measured steps carried him easily to the crest. Baldur was at his heels but I, for some reason, couldn't get a foothold in the sliding sand. I clambered, slid and scrabbled, feet going like pistons. Suddenly I felt extremely warm, as did the ground beneath me. I could *hear* strange rumblings—the volcanic mountain had become warm, and I knew it would pick this time to erupt, and I would be caught as in Pompeii. This unnerved me so completely that I relaxed, the best thing I could have done. The two wretches were sitting on the crest of the rim laughing at me. Baldur found it especially hilarious.

"Pull up the raincoat," he shouted.

What raincoat? I looked down and saw that the raincoat I had tied around my waist (to avoid carrying it) had worked loose down my legs. Every step I took on it was like walking on a slide. Sheepishly I hitched it up, flapped it over one shoulder and continued my climb. It was unthinkable to ask for help when a seventy-year-old man had made it unaided. A weary and wiser Amalia joined them in silence, and we three proceeded down the outer side, all in carefully measured steps. Hverfjall hasn't erupted again and one day I'll reclimb it, but not alone, for maybe geologists don't know as much as they think they do.

In the house, I've discovered that my hearing is excellent. And luckily, everything I hear is real. Above all the bedlam of the boys, there are times when I feel the vibration of a car before it passes and hear an airplane long before anyone else notices. I wish I didn't notice. The oil burner used to throw me into a queasy state as it rasped and wheezed and gurgled, and occasionally whined right up the scale. Later I discovered it is a good practice to turn off the heat when the tank is being filled, for the sandy sediment left by the Russian oil often works up into the filter. We also have our ageing automatic washer which was very sometimey until a new motor was put in. No one thought it necessary to bolt it to the floor, but it had to be perfectly balanced to spin-dry. Once, it wasn't level, and I watched that thumping monster walk twelve inches across the laundry floor toward me. It stopped walking in our new house, but it thundered and shook so much that on nervous days I wrung out the clothes by hand so I wouldn't have to listen. The dryer too had seen better days, and I had to push the barrel into a spin by hand for some weeks. The machine began to smoke, though only

I smelled it. Baldur thought I was really getting queer until one day we all saw the smoke coming up the steps from the cellar. I've been hanging out my clothes ever since, and my mind is much easier.

You might say that I am just not made for the Machine Age. Other people can approach a strange machine, read the label, and push the button. Not me. I read *all* the directions, the date and manufacturers' guarantee; mutter that despite assurances, no machine is perfect; and end up letting Baldur push the button. Even the kitchen stove has become an ordeal, for every time I touch a cooking pot I get a shock. It's probably my rubber-soled shoes on the plastic flooring, but why doesn't it shock someone else? I'm not that hot a number!

These experiences would probably not upset most people, but when a person's especially good hearing, sight, and sense of smell start working together under gloomy conditions, I think even the most stoic person will quiver. The night before Baldur's mother's funeral, these three faculties started working in me and all together.

Dusk had fallen long before we reached the farmhouse tired from our journey, and in that remote valley on a moonless night, the darkness was complete before we began dinner. No one lingered after coffee, for the women had to rise early for the funeral the next day, and Baldur was anxious to go visiting with his brother to a farm in the next valley.

Because of the overflow of relatives, we were given the front parlor to sleep in, a narrow couch to sleep on. I went to bed early and started to read. The sound of the truck mumbled into the distance and was absorbed in the wind, which now began a tentative exploration of the house. What had begun as shifting music on the telephone wires now slid into a scream, held it for an interminable moment, slackened abruptly, and shook the windowpanes.

I sat up straight in bed, straining to see beyond the shadows cast by the bedside candle.

The windows were black mirrors reflecting the limp velvet drapes and the wavery light. The organ with its cover closed, brooded darkly in a corner. It almost seemed about to peal forth a requiem for the dead—the woman, no longer a woman, who lay in the next room. I felt the presence of someone there beyond the French doors, almost at the foot of my bed. If the doors should open suddenly, what would I see? The closed coffin on the table, or a walking shroud? The carnations in the parlor, gay colored instead of white, exuded a cloying scent that almost nauseated me, and yet I liked carnations. Their odor filled the room, choking out the smell of my cigarette, and came in waves across the icy air.

A ripple of fear fingered the back of my neck as I stared. Iceland abounds with ghost stories, but people don't jeer at them, not here. I had laughed, of course. Imagine the stupidity of people who believed the dead could walk, who spoke of footsteps sounding audibly under a window when someone was about to die, but who saw no footprints. What of the tapping in the walls that came the moment the soul departed the body—a grave and awful sound, but *better to hear it than not.*

A faint perspiration appeared on my hands as I tore my eyes from the slit of darkness between those doors, and forced them back to my book. John Dickson Carr in a farmhouse in Iceland. Escape reading, guaranteed to thrill, but not to be read when alone in a strange house with no electricity.

The candle flame leaped, shuddered, streamed high and

thin. A draft must have caused it. A draft from an open door—or an opening one. If I looked up . . . nothing! The doors were still closed, glimmering whitely. No light in there, only darkness.

Then I heard a creaking noise of hinges, of someone moving on loose floorboards, someone in the dark passage outside the other door. I'd forgotten that other door which opened just at the end of the bed. I would not look. It was my imagination. I would read the words under the moist fingerprints on my book.

The creaking came again—from the hall. I drew the quilt over the shoulders of my thin nightgown and waited, eyes shifting frantically from the French doors to the now equally terrifying one leading to the passage. Under the wind's moan, I heard the soft brushing at the door and, before my distended gaze, the knob twisted slowly. The carnation scent hovered like a cold mist.

The door squealed open—as in an Inner Sanctum mystery, I thought hysterically. And the scene was right: midnight, an old isolated house, everyone asleep far upstairs, the keening wind, the murder story, the coffin in the next room, the heroine in nightdress. And the door opening slowly. I did not laugh now.

In the shadows of the hall I saw the grizzled head with unkempt beard, the pale, vacant eyes staring at me. My own eyes stared back transfixed. He began to mumble at me, inching the door wider.

He's harmless, I told myself. He had some sort of fever when he was twelve. He's just like a child, though he's an old man. He's really only twelve. *How old is twelve?*

He mumbled again, and I could not have understood the words had they been in English. Were his eyes as empty as they seemed? He was frowning now, under bushy brows, with a look of adult cunning.

There was nothing in the room to throw—no lamp, no heavy object, only soft kid slippers somewhere under the bed. And there was no place to run to if I dared, except through the pale French doors.

The carnation scent spilled over me in full force and I closed my eyes for a giddy instant. They flared open to see the door closing as interminably as it had opened, squeaking, groaning, then the thump, and the knob was released. A moment later I heard the creaking of boards as he moved down the hall and began to pace up and down, shuffling and mumbling. Outside the wind rose to a scream.

I picked up the book and began to read. My little gold watch said half after midnight. Baldur returned at two in the morning. What happened during that intervening hour and a half I'll never know.

Some years later I recounted this to an old friend in America. He too wondered about the carnations till I recalled the country custom in Iceland of postponing the funeral until the guests can gather by car or horseback. Embalming is not done in Iceland, hence the cold room and the carnations, which had lost their efficacy. The old man always paced at night and had only peeked in out of curiosity to see who was sleeping in the parlor. Perhaps he was as surprised as I was.

His sly look no longer deceives me, for *I* have spied on *him*. I have watched him finish his coffee, look furtively to left and right, then with practiced motion empty the bowl of lump sugar into his pocket, and smile wickedly to himself. Now we bring him candy when we visit and he hoards it jealously. He loves small children and guards them like a watchdog, muttering angrily if anyone rebukes them. When my Rikki goes to visit, the old man often comes to his room at night to pat him on the cheek; and during the day he often draws him into odd corners to conspire and whisper, "Have you got any candy?"

The unfamiliar, the unknown must always inspire a certain cowardice. Regaled with strange and unprovable tales, I have a great respect for the supernatural, unless I am writing. Then heaven help any spirit who knocks or raps, or any mortal!

By the way, did someone just open the door? I feel cold, sort of.

CHAPTER SIXTEEN

The Ruff and the Faithful

ALTHOUGH ICELANDERS ARE ALWAYS INTERESTED AND USUALLY quite willing to discuss matters of the supernatural, they are noticeably less voluble on the subject of religion. Certainly few people visit church between holidays except older people, and children attend Sunday school irregularly, if at all. Not that I believe churchgoing is necessary to faith but, with so many churches in existence and more being built, one would expect some amount of participation. Perhaps the fact that the Lutheran religion is state-supported deprives people of any real desire to participate. I hope that along with the modern style in church architecture will also come a modern approach to Bible teachings, for I have really missed the sense of communion and the refreshment received from my own Episcopal church services.

On the few occasions I have attended church, I have been unimpressed by the service and what I could understand of the sermon. It seemed there was nothing in it for me. I came to give, but nothing was expected from me.

Unlike the Episcopalians I was used to, the Lutherans do not kneel for prayers or bow their heads. If they feel respectful or humble, they conceal their feelings behind upright, expressionless faces. From what I saw of those around me, I feel that people go to church as an uncomfortable duty, prepared to watch a show. The choir sings, often quite beautifully, but the congregation is seldom asked to join in. They do not recite the prayers, but are prayed for; and it is the choir which makes responses, not the congregation. The priest, in his black robes and white seventeenth century ruff, preaches more to heaven than to the congregation, in a monotonous chant, as though there is indeed a wide cleft between him and the people for whom he is praying. I felt a discouraging lack of warmth even in the custom of filing out anonymously. I was used to the minister shaking each hand, making himself acquainted with each parishioner. And generally, as I remember, there were several waiting to discuss some point of his sermon. Here it seems the priest lays down the heavenly law and whether people accept, reject or understand it is not his concern.

Nationalism, as represented by the flag, and understandable when one remembers how recent is Iceland's status as an independent republic, is quite noticeable even in the church. In the three different churches in America which I visited, little if any emphasis was put on the flag. Here the Icelandic flag sometimes almost dwarfs the altar—that seems a bit presumptuous.

The strong nationalistic interest in Christianity, as it has been practiced in Iceland, is perhaps best portrayed in the stained-glass windows in the church at Bessastaoir. The church, which has been rebuilt several times since, was first constructed in 1,000 after Iceland's conversion to Christianity. Of the eight windows, commissioned in 1937 for the sixtieth birthday of President Ásgeir Ásgeirsson (whose official residence is close by), only two depict Bible stories; the main windows are about important events in the history of Christianity in Iceland. The first one shows the Irish Catholic monks who sought solitude here in 825. The second depicts the formal acceptance of Christianity by the Althing in 1,000, with the noted pagan chieftain who pleaded for its acceptance in the foreground. In the next three windows are pictured the last Catholic bishop of Iceland, the Lutheran bishop of Holar in northern Iceland who printed the first Bible in Icelandic, and the bishop of Skalholt, reputedly the greatest pulpit orator of Iceland. The sixth window is of Hallgrímur Pétursson, revered religious poet-priest. Relegated to corners are Christ delivering his Sermon on the Mount, and the Mother and Child. Similarly, the oldest paintings in the National Museum are also of early bishops and their wives, with Christ in the background.

Even to this day, Icelanders who can claim they are descendants of an early bishop or any cleric, do so with pride, for the most learned men of the old days were the clergy. It was the clergy also who served as the earliest teachers for those in outlying districts. Yet few traces remain in today's Lutheranism of the fervent Christianity practiced in the early years, and I have heard some cynics remark that if a man fails to earn a law or medical degree at the University, he can always pass the theology exam and gain some distinction.

From my own short experience at the University of Iceland, where I endeavored to learn a smattering of Icelandic, and from reports of Icelanders who have attended the University, I see that courses are taught in lecture style, and seldom does a student ask a question. This puzzled me for a long time. Apparently, I was the only dumb one in the class. (Of course a lot depends on whether the teacher is merely trying to transfer his knowledge, or whether he is trying to help his students understand the reasons for facts and give them tools for independent thinking.) Finally, I decided I could no longer pretend to understand and I began, and haven't stopped, asking questions. To my amazement, I found that there were others who did not fully understand, but who were too shy to ask because they hadn't been invited to do so. Perhaps because I am a woman, I find it extremely difficult to listen and absorb without questioning. An idea has little value unless I can toss it around and examine it a bit. But it seems very much the practice here for the teacher to conscientiously avoid pressing his opinions on the students, by treating everything impersonally and leaving them with a set of notes, a comfortable lack of curiosity and the privilege of believing or disbelieving what they have heard. I suppose and I hope that discussions are held outside the classrooms.

To return to my earlier point, I think the same impersonal attitude exists between priest and congregation, and since Icelanders have a horror of seeming to pry or of revealing their secrets (it's done instead by an undercover grapevine), it would be unthinkable for a priest to spend an afternoon visiting parishioners to inquire about their spiritual health. I have met only two priests whom I would consider inspired;

the others seem to have taken up the ministry as a business rather than a pursuit. One never seems to meet these men of the cloth outside of church and, during social occasions, they do not talk "shop." Although I haven't tried for some years, I believe that if I dropped in on an Icelandic priest to argue a point in theology, he would consider me unconventional and unfeminine to be interested in such things, and would feel much happier if I would talk with his wife, though his wife might be more interested in housekeeping than salvation.

Of three funerals I have attended here, only one seemed to bear any but accidental relation to the deceased. At only one did I glean from the priest's message any notion of a human being (who was incidentally not an Icelander) who had struggled and sought and achieved some measure of completion. At the others, I felt that the deceased was unknown to the priest except for his vital statistics. And at one of the funerals, pamphlets had been printed about the deceased person, almost like handbills. Afterwards, I felt like weeping when I saw these notices tossed on the seats or floor quite carelessly as the show was finished and people rushed to the exit, wearing an air of conventional gloom until they reached the street.

To begin at the beginning, one can expect to see a priest at a child's baptism. This is a vital occasion, for an expectant mother considers it bad luck even to discuss names for her child before its birth. When the child is born, it is listed as a male or female child in the hospital and census records. Not until the parents are ready for a ceremonial party does the christening take place, though it is usually done before the child is three months old. Until he is christened, the child is nameless, even to his parents, who will call him by some meaningless nonsensity until the day of the occasion. If baptism means so much, why does religion mean so little?

American children are usually named after they are conceived and mothers take delight in their approaching motherhood, or at least proclaim it as a fact. Not so the Icelandic girl who does not mention her condition until it becomes obvious, and to whom no one makes the observation until she has mentioned it herself, as though it is a matter of great shame. Pregnant women are seldom seen in public except when they are out shopping. For many years, other foreign wives and I were the only "inhabited ladies" who attended dances. Thank goodness, Baldur was not ashamed to be seen with me or to dance with me, though no other man would run the social risk of dancing with a fruitful flapper. Yet when the baby is born, it is the husband who pushes the carriage on the streets in a public assertion of his paternity. It is all very confusing.

When a child is confirmed, a priest makes his second important appearance in the life of an Icelander. The child's formal acceptance into the church is quite overshadowed, however, by the celebration which follows the event, making it more a holiday than a holy day. There is a family party, often with many guests, and parties among the newly confirmed set during the succeeding days.

Unless it's a civil ceremony, the priest appears again at the marriage ceremony, though some people never get around to making their wedlock either holy or civil. Gold wedding bands are exchanged at betrothal time, meaning that the couple are pledged, but have not yet set up housekeeping together. Diamond engagement rings do not exist as such. So far as the couple is concerned, after their engagement they are married in all but minor respects. I have been told that the single-taxation system for married people makes it impractical for young working couples to become formally married unless or until they can afford it.

Sometimes the christening of their first child is performed simultaneously with a couple's marriage ceremony. In one funny instance, the newspaper picture showed three sisters in white gowns and veils, marrying the three brothers of another family. Each happy bride carried her child, who was also baptized at the same time. It was a joyous and economical arrangement. So in addition to not asking, "What are you going to name the baby?" foreigners must not say to the pregnant young thing, "I suppose your husband hopes it will be a boy?" There may be no husband or fiancé. At least the father of the child, if his paternity can be proved, or the state will support the child until he is sixteen—a comforting thought for the young mother. And she, being under no social stigma, can lead her life much as before, especially if there is an older female relative in the house to care for the child.

A movement is being made these days toward more social activities centering around the church, not so much because the Church feels conscious of its social responsibility, but because it seems the Church might offer a steadying influence for the young people who have grown up in a world of easy money as compared with the struggles their parents have undergone. (Many teenagers earn a monthly salary for a summer job equal to that of their fathers'.) How this change will be effected and how effective it will be remain to be seen. The Church needs a new outlook if it is going to flourish.

The curious thing is that despite frequent exhortations to God Almighty and Jesus (and mostly by women; the men call on Hell and the Devil), I would say that Icelanders are a deeply religious people. It shows more in what they practice than in what they preach. They are tolerant to the nth degree; they are sincere in their respect for their own and others' responsibilities and rights; they don't look down on their fellows, only askance at their political differences; they accept indescribable hardship with fortitude and dignity; they *are* kind. While they don't go so far as to say, "It is God's will," they will shrug in their noncommittal way and say, "Þetta lagast," which means, surprisingly, "That will improve." One cannot call them optimistic in the usual sense, but if grim tenacity, acceptance of the ways of nature, and belief in their worth as Icelanders does not constitute optimism, it must mean a faith closely akin to that which we call "religious."

CHAPTER SEVENTEEN

The Light in the Winter

THE PROBLEM WE'VE HAD TO RESOLVE EACH YEAR IS HOW TO
spend Christmas. If I could spend Christmas Eve in America
and Christmas Day in Iceland, my life would be sweet.

Christmas Eve for me used to mean unbridled excitement,
stocking-hanging, clumsily but lovingly wrapped gifts under
the tree with their handmade Christmas cards, and going to
sleep with ears strained for the first tinkle of Santa's sleigh
bells. Later, it meant a quiet evening with the tree going up
beautifully, despite Daddy's forebodings, the lights on it
being lit for the first time, and a feeling of awe inside us all.
There were whispers and secrets, paper rustling, and Mother
playing carols on the piano while all of us sang. There were

unplanned, quiet talks, an appraisal of the year past, and thanks for being together at Christmas. The magic of Christmas Eve always remained, though Santa lost his enchantment, and Christmas Day itself became, depressingly, just another day.

Until our children grew old enough to appreciate Christmas, it was the loneliest time of year for me. Then, wonderfully, through them, it came to have meaning. Parents need children to make Christmas real, and children need parents to make it real for them.

Imagine my surprise when the holidays approached in Iceland to find that the former "quiet evening" was Christmas. The shops close at noon on Christmas Eve; the tree is up and the feast prepared, for Christmas in Iceland reaches its climax on the 24th, to be followed by twelve more days of merrymaking. Throughout Scandinavia the 24th is more celebrated than the 25th, but the holiday season in Iceland is one of the longest in any country. The preparations of cleaning and renovating the home, baking, and sewing new clothes occupy more attention here than buying gifts. And Christmas begins at 6:00 P.M. on the Eve as it did in the olden days.

In those times, when a man's castle was his turf hut, and the nearest neighbor was half a day's horseback ride away, mild fasting was observed during the thirteen days preceding Christmas to give the work-ridden housewife a yearly excuse for skimpy meals. During this season of long nights, children especially were urged to make things for themselves (to keep them busy, I suspect), since another custom was that everyone must have something new to wear on the holy evening or "the Christmas Cat will get you."

The thirteenth day before Christmas also marks the advent of Santa Claus, who takes the form of thirteen little dwarfs. These little men, supposedly the offspring of some vengeful crone in Icelandic mythology, appear each day, until on Christmas Eve, they are all present. The next day they begin to vanish singly and the holidays are not over until the the last has disappeared. Bearing such representative names as "pot licker," "bowl licker," "skýr glutton," "sausage stealer," "window peaker," and "candle glutton," to mention a few, their purpose is to steal food and naughty children. Though these mischievous little men still appear on Christmas cards, most parents have abandoned this fearful ruse to get the children to bed.

Though Christmas Eve was originally celebrated as a feast day, the festivities were not as elaborate as they are today. But there was a tree. In the country it was a wooden pole affixed to a crosspiece foot. Wires, notched for candles, sprouted from the pole and were covered with blackberry branches. Aside from the candles, the decorations were paper cornucopias made by the children and filled with candy. This was all made ready in the afternoon.

As dusk fell, the house was lighted with all available tallow candles (given to the children afterwards to celebrate the beginning of longer days and more light), as well as the customary home-made ones consisting of wicks propped in saucers of fish oil.

Then the family gathered together in the scrubbed common room, all wearing some new article of clothing. With the orgy of housecleaning, bathing, dressing and cooking over, the housewife went around to make sure that every corner of the house was illuminated, for who knew what evil spirit might lurk in a forgotten shadow! As she made this final inspection she might have chanted:

"Those may come who want to come
Those may stay who want to stay
Those may go who want to go
But don't harm me or mine."

After this powerful appeal, the evening could proceed. The
man of the house would read a Christmas sermon from a
book of lectures prepared for special occasions, a copy of
which was in every home, since going to church was usually
impossible.

Then followed the meal of boiled, smoked lamb, creamed
potatoes, turnips and unleavened, unsalted leaf bread (so
called because of its four-petal shape) followed by a dessert
of rice cooked in milk and served with cinnamon, sugar and
berry juice. Later in the evening came French-style pancakes sprinkled with sugar, and coffee. Some families fared
better on this feast day, but this is what Baldur remembers
about his early Christmases, and that was not even forty
years ago. On this day of days there must be no dancing,
arguing, card playing or hard language, for the devil was
watching.

Today, more work and a good deal more money go into
the preparations, and children and adults alike are often in
complete sets of new clothes on Christmas Eve. There are
hymns and sermons on the radio and a few might venture
out to church. The tree is different now too because it is a
real evergreen tree, which Icelanders appreciate for its own
form and decorate very simply. (The blue-lighted tree, thick
with tinsel and balls that we used to have has even been
replaced by a simpler version. Last year we strung yards and
yards of popcorn and glass beads around the tree from top

to bottom. Lit with a single string of colored lights, it was the happiest tree imaginable.) Though there are several gifts for everyone under the tree, the food is still the focal point of the evening.

Ptarmigan, beef, pork are served—the most expensive meats and fowl for those who observe American or English customs. Smoked lamb is also served, but often as a preview of the second-day meal, and the leaf bread still appears in many homes as a side dish. Christmas pudding still tops the meal, but with raisins added to the rice; then comes coffee sipped through a lump of sugar held on the tongue.

At this point, of course, the children's excitement can no longer be stifled, so there is a speedy exodus to the tree room. Five years ago under most trees there were handknit garments for everyone, a few plain toys bought at exorbitant prices and candy. Nowadays, ale and soda pop are served with the meal, gifts and candy are in profusion and are more often bought than made at home.

After the gifts have been exchanged, the family dances or rather marches around the Christmas tree, hand in hand, singing traditional folk or Christmas songs. With the small children, this dancing is apt to go on for hours and, in fact, continues whenever they encounter a Christmas tree during the remaining twelve days.

Evening coffee is the last big event with open sandwiches, cookies and cakes, notably "rjóma terta," which is a layer cake covered with whipped cream, and "pönukökur," the thin pancakes folded in pie-shaped wedges and bulging with whipped cream and jam. The children have soft drinks and cocoa, the latter still a luxury in most homes.

On Christmas Day, the children play with toys they only examined the night before, while the parents get a well-deserved late snooze, after which they receive guests or visit relatives. On the second day of Christmas, the 26th, there are dances and entertainment for grownups, while the third day is exclusively for children's parties at home or in public halls.

During the remaining days, everyone is presumably at leisure, and it's safer not to make office appointments before 11:00 A.M. New Year's Eve is a family night marked by displays of fireworks and bonfires—this is the only time they are legally allowed. Business resumes unenthusiastically after New Year's Day, but by the sixth of January everyone is relieved that the holidays are over, and that the Christmas tree, imported at the beginning of December and purchased locally a week before Christmas, can finally be thrown out.

Whether to have an American or Icelandic Christmas was our problem, resolved only recently by having both. So on Christmas Eve we have our feast, which means more to Baldur than all else. We dine at six as the Icelanders do, shining and scrubbed and wearing our best clothes (not new ones). We have the radio on for hymns, and enjoy our meal to the last swallow. Then we may drive out with the children to peek at the crèche in the Catholic church, or finish wrapping gifts. The boys bring their own gifts to the tree and hang their stockings, and then they can't hop into bed fast enough to hear Mamma's version of the Nativity and the Night Before Christmas. Though this should be a restful night for us, there are always a zillion things to do.

Sometime between four and six in the morning, little voices start chirping in the dark.

"Is it morning yet? Has he come? Look, here are the stockings!"

This is my signal to turn on the heat and start waking

Baldur. By the time everyone has found his slippers and bathrobe and been given cocoa and toast, and that vitally necessary coffee for us, the house is warm. We open our gifts by the lighted tree and Baldur and I spell each other for sleeping while the children carry on. Dinner at noon consists of the warmed-up remains from the night before, but afternoon coffee is fabulous, whether at home or visiting. In this way we have made Christmas stretch over two days—a happy solution for all.

Until the boys are old enough to read this book, they won't know that Icelandic children are receiving gifts when *they* are hanging stockings; nor will their chums know that while they are still sleeping off Christmas Eve, our boys are opening their gifts in the only lighted house on a dark street. It's only a matter of time, but we're enjoying our two-day Christmas while we can. Last year the following bedtime conversation was overheard:

"Do you think there really is a Santa Claus?"

"No. Do you?"

"Well, I guess there isn't." Pause. "Are you going to sleep the way we're supposed to, anyway?" Very long pause.

"Maybe we'd better. Just to be sure."

CHAPTER EIGHTEEN

I Remember You

ASIDE FROM CHRISTMAS EVE, WHICH IS PRIVATE, ALMOST ALL
the holidays in Iceland are observed in much the same way:
by home entertaining, and, specifically, a coffee party. The
usual holidays are observed by flags at half or full mast in
every other house yard, and extra baking for the housewife.

The 17th of June, which commemorates Iceland's final
independence from Denmark in 1944, is the one festive day.
Parades in the morning are followed by trips to town in the
afternoon, when the streets are thronged with people. The
midtown streets are roped off from traffic, and amidst candy,
ice cream and balloon booths are several orchestras which
play folk or popular music for dancing in the streets till midnight. Most of the afternoon is devoted to political speeches

and formal addresses by various statesmen and gymnastic exhibitions by school children. This is the only holiday of the year on which people are not expected to serve coffee to guests.

Hallowe'en, Thanksgiving Day and Valentine's Day do not exist, naturally. Mother's Day and Father's Day were inaugurated (if that is the word) several years back and recently Wife's Day, when husbands are urged, via newspaper ads, to bring flowers to their wives to make them happy. (My spouse swept the floors and helped clear the dinner dishes as a bonus for me last year.)

The three local holidays most enjoyed are on three consecutive days of February, the third coinciding with the beginning of Lent. On Bun Day, the children flail their parents out of bed with crepe-paper wands, each blow earning them one cream-filled bun (which the mother bakes or buys) at coffee time. That evening, dried peas are set to soak for Bursting Day on the morrow, when everyone is supposed to eat as much salt meat and peas (boiled together) as he can hold. On Ash Day, little girls fasten bags of ashes on male pedestrians, without being caught, and little boys fill their tiny bags with pebbles to be affixed to ladies. The first time this happened to me, I was unaware of the custom and a little annoyed, for the children jump away if you're looking. Neither did I like their stealthy pursuit or mystifying laughter. Now I enjoy the day, except for having to sew enough of those fascinating little bags for all the children. And often as not, the small ones find their bags so precious, they won't risk hanging them on anyone but themselves.

After Confirmation, little attention is paid to birthdays outside the close family, though the husbands like to observe theirs. It is not advancing age that makes women neglect celebrating their own birthdays, but very often the work involved. A mother prepares fetes for her family, but on her own day it seems so incongruous for her to make her own party that she is glad to let it pass unnoticed. However, when a woman reaches fifty, even she agrees to the public recognition of her birthday, for from the age of fifty a person in Iceland really feels acclaimed. His birthday party is often an extravagant affair beginning in the afternoon and extending far into the night. No one is specifically invited, but all those who know or love the person may come from afar to this reunion of kinfolk and friends who may not have met for years. Relatives from abroad even plan their home-coming visits at a birthday time, if possible.

We attended a sixty-year birthday party of a friend at Myvatn in northern Iceland, and the celebration was unforgettable. About a hundred guests of all ages, though mostly adults, were ranged at long tables before a fabulous array of cakes, breads and coffee. Then, one after another, guests rose to speak. Some had written poems for the occasion, extolling the hostess, and each reading brought a round of spontaneous applause. Most guests spoke of the hostess and the circumstances under which they had met her. As one story followed the next, the almost forgotten threads of the woman's life were woven together. Former next-door neighbors, schoolmates, business acquaintances and old friends who had traveled long distances told little stories illustrating the admirable qualities or pleasant memories of the hostess. One very old man, bedridden for months, had gotten up, put on his rusty blacks and tottered in on his cane, for he wouldn't have missed the birthday of an old friend for any sickness. Our hostess sat at the head of the table listening and the tears streamed down her face unchecked. Even her husband was misty-eyed at this salutation given her. Certainly no one in Iceland can ever feel forgotten when he has such an anniversary. Birthday parties like these should be held for every American who feels he is a forgotten failure, and he would find, surprisingly, that more people than he dreamed knew him and remembered him kindly.

People in America, it seems, hate to count their years after a certain age, for old age has become synonymous with senility and uselessness; and the enforcement of retirement age at sixty-five seems to have contributed to this feeling. Housewives deplore their loneliness and the never-ending housework but, because the old-fashioned family unit is out of favor in modern America, most women would find it more intolerable than their loneliness to have an elderly relative live in.

Iceland still has no appreciable problem with its aged, perhaps because old people are not considered to be a problem. For the most part, Iceland keeps her old folks at home and it has been a pleasant and profitable arrangement for everyone.

Today's senior citizens spent their younger and middle years in times when there were few material comforts. Upon retirement, they have no pattern of prosperous living to maintain, and their small demands can usually be met by pensions and a share of the wages of a younger member of the family.

Through the Old Age Pension Act of 1900, to which all farm and unskilled workers subscribed (at that time 90 per cent of the people were engaged in farming), and through other pension systems for seamen, government workers, teachers and trade union members, the older folk are assured of a moderate income.

They also benefit from state medical insurance, which is compulsory for everyone, and which covers hospitalization, except in cases of chronic invalidism. Thus for a monthly payment of $1.20 per person over sixteen, one pays only about $.13 per visit to his family doctor (who may also be a specialist), his eye doctor, and his ear, nose and throat specialist. (Specialists visited on one's own may charge from $2.00 to $5.00.) Medical insurance even covers up to two-thirds of the cost of medicines. It also pays for the full cost of childbirth in state hospitals and about two-thirds of the expense of a private nursing home. Prenatal care is free in the competent but overcrowded state clinic, though many expectant mothers prefer private doctors despite their special fees. Icelandic women seem to take pregnancy in a casual manner and, barring complications or the unique phenomenon of the first baby, they and I often get extra vitamins, calcium and iron pills from their family doctor, and confine their checkups to a minimum three visits during the latter part of pregnancy. This medical assistance plan is common to all and reciprocal among all Scandinavian countries, so that an Icelander may move to Norway, for example, and immediately enjoy the medical benefits he received in Iceland.

It is a wonderful plan for patients even though, because there are no private appointments, one may have to wait one or two hours for each office visit. The doctors manage to make a living, but nothing like the heights they could achieve under the American system of private practice. Yet when you consider what most people earn annually, the low fees the doctors charge are not way out of line. (Factory workers and teachers *alike* earn about $2,000 annually; skilled workers, $2,500; engineers, $2,500 to $3,000; doctors and dentists, $4,000, not including the expenses of equipment, cars and their offices.)

The family in Iceland looks after its own as a matter of course. When parents are left alone, they often keep house well into their 70's and support themselves, or they may be supported by their children, who also help out by house-cleaning, shopping and nursing when necessary. The old person wants to remain physically independent as long as possible, but the assumption is that when he can no longer do so, there is a place for him in his son's or daughter's home.

When the widowed partner moves in, if it is the wife who has outlived her husband, she makes herself busy in a variety of ways, for though she expects her children to welcome her, she also expects to contribute as much as possible to the welfare of the family. Thus she shares the housework, as her strength allows, baby-sits, and does plain and fancy hand-work like darning, knitting and crocheting, and sometimes spinning and weaving. Several shops in Reykjavik do a brisk business in handmade goods. Since there is a growing market abroad for these products, the skills of the old may become quite profitable. The work a dependent mother or mother-in-law does in many cases releases the daughter for part-time employment, and in all cases it lightens her household duties, and provides her with the companionship to which so many Icelanders are used.

A large precentage of histories in memoir form about certain localities, as well as books of poetry and philosophy, are written by men who have "retired."

In such a child-parent relationship, two ideas are clearly recognized: that each party be as independent as possible, and that the authority in the house be the son or daughter. Because of this mutual respect for rights, problems of in-law interference seldom reach the point of incompatibility. The aged parent has his own room, usually apart from the main life of the family to ensure privacy. But he is included in all family affairs and receives friends in his own room or the living room. Then the daughter of the house helps prepare coffee and is often part of the group, for the topics of conversation of the aged are also of interest to the younger married.

In social groups, the old person is not made to feel unimportant and useless, and is respected for his age. His interest in general subjects is keen and he joins in discussions with gusto. His opinions, despite the deference paid them, are never imposed on others, and are as open to contradiction and correction as those of anyone else in the group.

There is one large and several smaller old folks' homes in Reykjavik, in addition to one for retired seamen, who cannot or prefer not to live with their children. Most of the people living in them are infirm to some extent. These homes will probably increase in number during the next years, for with the mushrooming population of Reykjavik, apartments are necessarily smaller than the rambling farms and older houses.

Modern Reykjavikans have pulled slightly away from tradition by more often living alone, but once they are alone, they spend much of their time visiting their relatives.

CHAPTER NINETEEN

Becoming a Round Peg

IN SOME OF MY WISTFUL MOODS, IT OFTEN SEEMS THAT COMING to live in Iceland has meant only giving up things. Sometimes I feel I have given up so much I don't know who I am any more.

Most women give up their names when they marry, so that is nothing new. The Icelandic woman doesn't do this, however, but remains the daughter of her father, in this patriarchal country, until the day she dies—causing agonies of confusion if she travels abroad with her spouse under her own name.

We foreigners give up our countries, too, in some respects. Shortly after my arrival here, we visited a theatre with friends. It must have been a special occasion for at one point the orchestra played "God Save the King." A friend whispered helpfully to me that that was the British National Anthem. "It isn't," I retorted with unexpected tears. "It's My Country 'Tis of Thee." When I first left America, I brought with me a small American flag and a jarful of American soil. It sat on a bookcase in our house for a long time before I outgrew the need for proclaiming myself American.

We do not give up our American citizenship as other foreigners must do when marrying Icelanders, but we are regarded as quasi-Icelanders by the Americans. We acquire Icelandic citizenship and are subject to the same laws as though we were born here, but to Icelanders we are Americans.

We give up our language when coming here to stay. This is not compulsory, but necessary, unless we want to live in isolation forever. So much pressure is put on one to use Icelandic that in time one forgets how to express himself in English. After years of using simple and familiar words of English with Icelanders who want to speak English, it comes as a shock to hear articulate Americans speak what we once took for granted. After a while most of us here begin to speak a strange combination of English and Icelandic, and have great difficulty separating the two even in daily speech. (I've noticed that all foreigners speaking Icelandic are much more readily understood by other foreigners than by Icelanders—I guess because foreigners make the same kinds of mistakes.) Luckily, many books in English are translated into Icelandic, and books in both languages can be bought in the bookstores. Also, more than half the moving pictures are American or English, though the reaction to them is not.

A visit to the movies in Iceland requires some attention

for, after all these years, I still feel hopelessly American
at a movie theatre. In the first place, there are no double
features. Sometimes there is a month-old newsreel or an
animated cartoon, occasionally a short subject, and always a
preview of the next film. On weekends there is a 3:00 P.M.
showing for children and some theatres have a regular
5:00 P.M. showing of "Tarzan," "Zorro," "Roy Rogairs" (hard
g), etc. The 7:00 and 9:00 P.M. showings are for adults and
children under thirteen are forbidden if there is much violence and sex, or children under fifteen if there is only the
normal Hollywood amount. All picture houses are the size
of American local theatres, but they show to disadvantage
3-D, Todd A-O and Cinemascope films. (There must be a lot
of determined or nearsighted people in Iceland.)

At 8:50 then, one enters a lobby of milling enthusiasts.
They smoke, stare at one another unblinkingly, regard themselves in the mirrors, and the young men adjust their hairdos.
Some buy candy, some read the translated summary of the
film from the pamphlets which are obtained freely from the
ticket office, while other people are reading yet another
newspaper. (All newspapers are tabloid size and carry about
one-third foreign news.) Suddenly the inner doors of the
lobby sweep open, and there is a noiseless jostle to get inside,
which is strange since all seats are reserved. Silently everyone files in and sits down. The ladies keep on hats and coats,
but may unbutton the coat and remove their gloves when
the house lights go off. The men make a to-do of whipping
off their overcoats and folding them carefully before sitting
down with said bundles. There is muted conversation while
advertisement slides are flashed on the screen to the accom-
paniment of recorded dance music.

At 9:00 the lights dim, the curtains ripple apart grandly,

and the title of the film comes on. After that and before the opening of the story come the knots of people who have been waiting outside but who are either too shy to enter in full light, or too blasé to hurry for a single feature. They now stampede down the aisles, confer with the sweater-girl ushers, then force rows of people to stand so they can sidle by—facing the injured parties with apologies while butting the heads of those in the row ahead. Most seats are spring seats, so there is a deal of coordination required before everyone gets comfortable again. Finally all is serene and only the furtive rustle of cellophane competes with the film.

Whether the story has a thrilling chase, hair-raising horrors, side-splitting laughs, stark tragedies or simple, masterfully acted scenes, there is not a gasp, giggle, tear or sigh from the audience. There is the crinkle of cellophane. I don't believe I am a noisy person, but I do have to express my feelings in the movies, and it doesn't bother me at all when my sudden laughter echoes alone. If I hear another chuckle in the distance, it is almost always another foreigner who also got the point. Only three times have I heard paroxysms of laughter—once during a Danny Kaye film, again during "Sitting Pretty" (which has been imported three times), and a third time, to my surprise, during a made-for-export film from America which showed a series of strippers stripping. I didn't laugh at that one, only slunk down in my seat and wished fervently that America would reimport this sort of film along with some of their other frilly and phony extravaganzas, and send more of the well-acted films that are still being made on low budgets for regular-size screens.

Whatever inner responses the movie arouses are quickly masked by the audience during the final scene, when there

is a hurried buttoning of coats, sliding into gloves and overcoats. The second the lights go on, there is a mad dash for
the door, the exodus being in utter silence. Even stray half-
smiles are replaced with graveness, and no one but me cries
uncontrollably, "Oh, *wasn't* that wonderful!" Unfortunately,
once the words are spoken in English, the abrupt turning
of heads recalls me to Iceland, and I too stalk out grimly
while the recorded dance music plays on.

I said that women give up their names in marriage. This
Americans accept as a custom, but pity the foreign settlers
who come to Iceland. Here they are required by law to
translate their names into the Icelandic counterpart or
change them entirely if they are untranslatable. This is done
to insure the purity of the language. Icelanders stake their
integrity on translating every conceivable word into Icelandic. How must it be for those who by changing their names
really start their lives anew?

Another thing we may give up is the tradition of Sunday
morning. Ah, that used to be a lazy time! A late breakfast
of bacon and eggs and warmed-up beans from Saturday
night's dinner was shared by a bathrobe-clad family. There
was a thorough reading and shuffling of the Sunday papers,
followed by speedy preparations for church, if anyone was
going. Around noon came a lackadaisical cleaning of the
house while Mother tended her plants and made dinner preparations. During all this, various church services were tuned
in on the radio. Mother sang beautifully as she went about
her chores, but Daddy knew all the words of all the hymns
and sang with more vigor than tune. Dinner was at 3:00
with all hands setting and clearing the table and washing
up. From 4:00 on, we went our own ways, but Sunday mornings remained an oasis in the week of routine and school.

Here in Iceland the nation eats at noon in accordance with weekday appetites and the lazy time is out, except for husbands. Breakfast is a snatched affair, sandwiched between dressing children, housecleaning, buying the milk and starting dinner. The Sunday papers, all tabloid size, contain no comic sections. (Funny, that this is the first thing every American wife in Iceland misses. It may prove we are not an intellectual group, but it also proves that we like to laugh. The daily papers include a four-drawing comic strip of "Ferdinand," or a mediocre gangster strip, painstakingly translated. [E.g. "Slip me the gat; I'm gonna get the dame" becomes, "Give me the gun; I am going to capture the girl."] Only one paper so far has managed to run a full page of color comics once a week, and the children clip and save those twelve squares of "Ferdinand" and twelve of the "Katzenjammer Kids" [which would be quite incomprehensible to Icelanders without translations.]) At high noon on Sunday we eat, while the radio holds forth with news and singing sopranos. There is little opportunity for table conversation, as is indeed the case every other day, for the news is timed to come on during dinner and supper.

After dinner, all hands do not clean up. The older children may go to the weekly children's film (shown on Sundays, not Saturdays, presumably because school is held on Saturday) at the neighborhood theatre, or we may all take a short drive in the car. Generally I beg off from the drive and relish the prospect of an uninterrupted hour, during which I can finish cleaning, bake a cake, write home or look through the papers myself.

This is the time when Anne Lindbergh suggests that women organize their thoughts and refresh their souls. Sometimes I go for weeks without having my soul refreshed, for it's difficult to achieve that receptive frame of mind at a moment's notice and there are always interruptions. I used to snatch time by rising at six, but at least one of the children would join me in surprised pleasure. Now I shall wait, as presumably Mrs. Lindbergh did, till my children all go to school at the same time, or at least until they all go to school. I think it would not be too untrue to say that Icelandic housewives, if not young mothers everywhere, find the pace most hectic on weekends.

We give up our families to whom we are dear and become the foreign "in-law." Husband suddenly becomes not only husband, but brother, sister, friend and parent. This is quite a load of responsibility for an innocent Icelander who thought he was bringing back a wife who could quickly stand on her own feet and go the separate way of women in Iceland. The foreign wife has been a companion to her husband before coming to Iceland and behaves in the same way after her arrival here, whereas the Icelander, having behaved as the Romans do in Rome, returns to Iceland, sheds most of his foreign-acquired ease, and behaves as the Icelanders do, to the incredulity and resentment of his wife. He sees Icelandic wives off in groups, in sewing or card clubs, and wishes his wife would do the same. He may not realize that most of these ladies' circles stem from school days and do not readily accept outsiders, even Icelandic, except as occasional guests. Although I would not call it an "organization-conscious" country, Iceland is very cliquish.

Foreign wives may be lucky in their relations with Icelandic relatives. Much depends on how affluent, and therefore how relatively modern, their in-laws are, and how close the husband is to his mother. One mother may present a gift to a daughter-in-law; another will insist on her son sitting by her till she falls asleep at night. One mother may go on polishing her son's shoes and serve him (but not his wife) breakfast in bed, though the wife has decided that polishing shoes is a man's personal job, and breakfast in bed a reciprocal luxury between husband and wife. One mother may deplore publicly the fact that her husband has married a foreign woman, while another will believe and announce that her son has done well. I have been lucky in my in-law relationships. Even though when I came, ideal wifely behavior meant old-European coddling, I must say that I stopped laying out slippers and pipe, and polishing shoes when I saw that my favors were accepted neither with surprise nor thanks. Whether or not wives accord with in-laws, it is easier for them to make friends with other foreigners or with Icelanders who have been "out" often enough to feel at home anywhere.

I write this about foreign wives, but I have no idea how the foreign husbands of Icelandic women make out. There are a few such couples living and employed in Reykjavik, though most are American civilians working at Keflavik. In this masculine society, how can a man feel himself a man when his wife has to lead him around!

In coming to Iceland, we give up certain social courtesies which Americans take for granted. There is no "ladies first" tradition nor little, if any, rising of men when women enter a room. A man doesn't help a woman on with her coat, unless it's his wife, and unless she asks him. (What's the matter with her; can't she put on her own coat?) In fact, at a party it is more often the hostess who helps both men and women with their wraps, and the hostess who lights everyone's cigarette.

I would collapse if anyone but Baldur offered to carry a

heavy bundle for me. An American lady I know who was retrieving an empty suitcase she had lent someone was offered and accepted help in carrying it from a male acquaintance who had been "out." He carried the suitcase one block through midtown Reykjavik. Within half an hour of her arrival home, three women telephoned to mention the fact and to inquire tactfully about her marital happiness.

Men and women, the former especially, go to a party to be entertained, with little thought of exerting themselves to be entertaining. They are not brought up to help others enjoy themselves, so that the first half hour of any gathering is apt to drag.

But I've found a way to squash people who telephone and ask imperiously, "What number is this?" as though it's *my* fault. I say sweetly, "What number are you calling?" I can be cagey, too. And I can be icily formal when someone, usually a man, shouts "Hah!" on the telephone, when he means "I'm sorry, I don't understand you" or "Will you please say that again?"

We give up these little courtesies which make life pleasant, but they are, after all, small losses.

It is a curious fact that those of us who arrived ten years ago may have given up forever a young way of life we might still be enjoying abroad.

When I came, married couples stepped automatically into an age-old mold of settled habits, where fun for married people meant stylized coffee parties with everyone gathered in a ring, only leaving his chair when coffee was served, after which he returned to the same chair. More than one foreign woman had the feeling of stepping backward in time and forward in age. Now, in the 1960's, Iceland has in many ways reached the sort of level we enjoyed in America when we left. But we are ten years older and cannot go ahead as though we never left off. The group now starting ahead is not our group; ours is becoming the "older generation" bound invisibly to the past.

Iceland has made a jump toward modernity in fifteen years which older countries have achieved only in fifty years. Materially, Iceland never had it so good, and many comforts are available if one has the money to buy them. Housing is better than ever and always more buildings and shops are being erected all the time. Roads, traffic, some degree of zoning are all converging to prepare for an even greater expansion of the capital city. And all men, from architects to carpenters, connected with the building trade are working full time.

It's another matter for professional people like doctors and engineers who have trained abroad at some length and at relatively great expense. Despite the strides made toward material well-being, they find that they are far ahead of their times, trained beyond their usefulness. Doctors complain of too few hospitals where they can continue to learn, of woefully inadequate equipment, of no time or money for refresher courses. Engineers find that only ideas useful to the building boom or the fishing industry are in favor. There is no place for many of these men. It would have been as well for them to have limited their training to the University of Iceland for the people, as represented by the government, are simply not interested in investments for either science or research. Those men studying abroad are privately advised not to come back, for they will only stagnate here while they work overtime, and they will have to accept one-third the salary they could command abroad. And why should they return! These bitter brilliants can find little comfort in the thought that they are spearheading a movement that will be a reality in ten more years. They want to fulfill themselves now. But for them, the time is not now.

Progress has become a tenable theory, but interpreting it and adapting it to the real needs of an "independent" country requires a fundamental change in outlook.

This is a day when timeworn methods are outdated, but old habits still cling, and we who came here too soon, or returned too soon, must live along with them. A fresh new wind is stirring for those who are coming now. The twenty-year-olds will feel its breezes, and our children will know no other. For some of those in their forties and fifties, it is a chill, disturbing wind which makes them draw their old coats tighter in protection. I wonder how many of them realize this, or care; or caring, could change.

This, the expectation of living a full life, is the hardest thing to give up, because we do not give it up; it is taken from us.

CHAPTER TWENTY

When Am I Leaving?

AS FAR AS LEAVING THEIR COUNTRY IS CONCERNED, THE FEW Icelanders who emigrate do so not to escape tyranny or to find democracy in action, but to find a specialized job that suits them and/or pays more money. Iceland has always put more value on qualities than on material things; hence, the hold of the motherland, and it's a strong hold.

Despite my many adverse criticisms, I find to my amazement that when I return to America, I am hotly in defense of Iceland. Only when visiting America am I aware of how much I have changed.

As mentioned before, when I first came, I worked as a newspaper correspondent, and then suddenly I lost my "nose for news." My perspective had gone and I could no longer view Iceland through totally American eyes. My horizons narrowed to four walls, four children and one husband. During the first six years I made three trips home with the children, and was glad to be "home." After an interval of five years, I went again to "the States," not "home"; and the transformation was as complete as it ever will be, for I saw America through foreign eyes.

The speed of life bewildered me, as well as the reasons for the necessity of such speed. The noise, the dirt seemed overpowering at first, and on dark streets I did not fear winds or ghosts, but flesh-and-blood attackers of the two-or four-footed variety (dogs are not allowed in Reykjavik). People seemed friendly on the surface but suspicious underneath. They seemed to place too much importance on what Icelanders consider trifles. The variety of foods was staggering, and yet I lost weight in three months. If you have accustomed yourself to food as a filler, it is difficult to make a choice when so much is offered. I had longed for a hot fudge sundae but, with ice cream sold in every shop, it wasn't "special" any more. I had remembered the gay throngs at movie houses, but television has changed all that. Now there is little reason to dress up and feel you're part of "people" again. The air was sultry and enervating; the trees seemed smothered with their own density. I longed for a breath of fresh, cool air—I who loved heat and who hugged a tree on my first visit back to America!

On the other hand, the abundance of clothes and the gadgets to make the housewife's job easier did make me envious. I strolled alone, loving the laughter on the streets, the greetings of barbers, policemen and bus drivers, people chatting unconcernedly, confident in their casual attire, their bare arms and legs and the endless styles of *shoes*. I felt the wild exhilaration of salt air and hot sun at the beach, the whisper and rustle of rain through the leaves of maple trees, and experienced that strange poignancy of a summer evening when the air is a caress instead of a blast—a painful, young-at-heart feeling, though I knew that seventeen was a long time ago.

I do have regrets, but I can't imagine my life as otherwise than it is. I am more Icelandic than American, and have found resources of strength in myself which I believe would never have been tapped in America.

There is a refreshing simplicity in grappling with realities rather than fighting in a fog, of being a discernible fish in a small puddle rather than a rivet in a gigantic machine. America is rich with promise, sometimes forthcoming, sometimes not, and you can fall hard. Iceland promises nothing. You may get little, but you appreciate what you have. If you get nothing, there is no place to fall. Life is not so exciting as in America (it's often dreadfully boring), but the more leisurely pace makes it easier on the nervous system. There is no saving philosophy for the individual in the American system, so far as I can see; Iceland's fatalism may be a negative philosophy, but it makes for survival and it is tempered by a real belief in the dignity of man.

Even the bare landscape grows on one, as does Oriental art: and appreciation of its beauties depends on the capacity of the onlooker. Here again, you have to work for what you get.

Yet there are many things I would like to see changed in Iceland:

I wish people were more casual, less inhibited in public, would not stare so unabashedly, and would tone down their radios.

I wish that low-priced fruits and vegetables were more abundant, that clothes and other merchandise were more varied in price (not just uniformly high); or perhaps I should reverse this and say that I wish salaries paid government workers were commensurate with their abilities.

I wish there was home milk delivery, for our daily purchase of four to five bottles at 3.7 pounds per bottle is heavy to carry along with other purchases. I wish that candy factories would discontinue a few brands of cream chocolate and concentrate on milk chocolate instead, and with peanuts instead of almonds. I wish that the elegant restaurants would order machines for making ice cream which would be as effective as the frozen-custard machines. Icelandic ice cream seems to consist of frozen slivers of cream, unsalted, barely sweetened, and inadequately flavored, if at all. I wish canned corn, baked beans and spaghetti were not luxury-priced items. (Recently I read a cynical report of a foreign correspondent who stated grimly that on the entire flight to wherever he was going, he was fed only canned beans and Spam. My heart bled with envy for him.) Ah, foolish dreams! Spinach, stringbeans, pumpkin for pie, green peppers, canned tomatoes, summer squash, cornmeal, fresh young beets, poultry seasoning, turkey—that would be living it up! (Every time I tried to buy chicken in the stores, I got blank looks. Now I ask for hen and get it. In the cookbooks are dozens of recipes for chicken, but only one for fowl: boil until tender.)

I wish there were something like the Good Housekeeping Institute here to test foods and other products before they appear on the market to aid housewives in making wise selections. I wish that Icelandic recipes would specify oven temperature and baking time, instead of saying, "bake until done."

I wish that in the dark winter, husbands, school children, babies, and therefore mothers, were not expected to rise before dawn to get cracking, and that wives were entitled to base pay not meant for everlasting food bills. I wish that foreigners were exempt from customs duties at Christmas time. Icelandic grandparents can send gifts to their grandchildren, but gifts from foreign grandparents are not so Christmasy when up to 100 per cent duty must be paid on their value.

I wish Icelandic artists could conceive of women as something other than bodies. In case any reader thinks I exaggerate about the position of women in Iceland, let him read page 55 of the 1961 pocket *Memory Book*. Under the title, "Pregnancy Periods of some Animals," is a list beginning with "asses" and ending with "women." I wish I didn't sputter helplessly at that! (Interesting to note that the whale's pregnancy period approximates the human woman's—if I may take the liberty of calling women human. And, by the way, is the time of gestation for a woman supposed to jog the memory and/or conscience of men? Women are generally quite aware of the length of this period.)

I wish more streets were paved and more sidewalks were in existence, so that shoes would last longer, children could play safely, and pedestrians could live longer. I wish that uninvited sheep and horses would not wander up our driveway to graze on our baby trees or in our trash barrels. I wish streets and house numbers were clearly and consecutively marked so that strange ladies would not burst into our house, saying, "Is this the maternity home?" when I'm not even expecting.

I wish main streets would be marked so for drivers like me, instead of the negative "stop" signs on side streets; that reasonable speed limits would be established so that the law-abiding car-crawler wouldn't seem like a stick-in-the-mud. I could wish that taxis and buses would not drive so fast, but a lot of good that would do!

I wish people here liked masked balls, cookouts, charades, private theatricals, and double-dating for expensive occasions, and that one man would not grandly insist on paying the bill for a whole table of drinkers, and cause his guests to wonder how they can ever repay the obligation. This paying of others' bills is not an Icelandic custom; it must be a foreign import.

I wish some enterprising money-maker would open a newsreel theatre in the center of town, open all day for those with a half-hour bus wait, or for those whose free time comes in the afternoons when no theatres are open. Since Icelanders read an average of two papers and listen to two or three newscasts daily, a theatre which offered news and short subjects and cartoons would be heavily patronized. And if the Icelandic government decides to open its own TV reception station, I hope they will bear in mind that the Huntley-Brinkley news team would not injure Iceland's culture a bit.

Since the national economy is always strained, I wish we could limit the importation of paper and tin by saving newspapers and magazines for reprocessing, by flattening and saving tin cans as Americans did during the war years. This would make the trash collector's job much easier too, and here in Kópavogur his license number is second only to the mayor's, making him a V.I.P.

In this my adopted country, I would be tempted to give up American citizenship if I could be as gladly for some political leader as I was madly for Adlai but, sadly, I can't. Someone has said that Iceland is run by lawyers, which is all to the good for legalizing procedures, but a hindrance to positive action and practical idealism.

This list of wishes and queries might continue indefinitely, but in another ten years many of these wishes will be realities. Some are changing now. There are other things I hope will not change:

I hope the country custom of serving food and cakes on platters and endless coffee for a fixed price will endure. I do not like this measuring out of portions and serving coffee by the cup.

Icelandic coffee is the best I've ever tasted, though a foreign coffee exporter said that Iceland imports second-class coffee. When I took coffee with me to America recently, my father pronounced it "Excellent. It tastes like *real* coffee," he added. One cup of it is never enough. For one thing, coffee here is made by dripping it through a cloth bag, and it is never allowed to boil.

Some find it macabre, but I find it beautifully serene to see the Fossvog church graveyard gleaming with lights at Christmas. That the dead seem to rejoice with the living is a satisfying thought.

Although midtown traffic is as bad during business hours as in any city, it was not so long ago that a stream of cars halted, for too long, I thought, to allow a mother with small boy to cross the street. As I came abreast of them, the two had reached the curb, but motorists waited in amusement until the boy's toy duck, rolling after him at the end of a three-yard string, also made the curb in safety. Another time, traffic was held up by an out-of-town jeep, parked in the middle of the street. Its owner could be seen on the stoop of a house to which he had apparently just brought a sack of potatoes from the country. Not a car honked as the old fellow offered the potatoes and the housewife exclaimed and shook his hand vigorously. From the pantomime we could imagine that she asked of other news from the country, then shook hands again and thanked him, while he shook her hand vigorously, said it was a pleasure, and sent his greetings to the rest of the family.

In the first instance, you might say that the child's duck was a traffic hazard and mutter, "Why doesn't that kid get off the street!" But the comment here would more likely have been, "Well, well, the little fellow brought his duck to town," with no sarcasm implied. In the second instance everyone realized what a blessing it is to receive potatoes from the country, and how necessary to have a moment to chat and to thank. Maybe such tolerance is old-fashioned, but I'm glad it happens here.

Last fall, I saw some drapery material that seemed made for our house, but was beyond our immediate means. Two months later, I was able to purchase it with an unexpected windfall, and was about to sew on the last length when I discovered on closer examination that each length had one rotten tear or more. I was exhausted at having spent two days and nights making the curtains, matching the pattern, sewing long seams on my foot treadle machine, and angry at the price we had paid for this defective material. We took it back to the store. The happy result was that the owner not only gave us a 50 per cent discount on the cloth, but remade all the drapes for me, and eliminated by repair the two weak points that remained. Could anything have been more fair? And yet the fact that she had won our goodwill obviously did not interest her nearly so much as that she had done her duty as she saw it.

A farmer we know recently refused the offer of a seat in the Althing (Iceland's Congress). As he is undoubtedly held in great respect in his district, we wondered why he had refused what most would consider an honor.

"I'm a farmer, not a politician," he said. "If I had to just sit and listen for three hours a day, who would run the farm? No, I'm too busy." There is a man who knew what he wanted and had the resistance to take it.

They tell a story here of an old farmer who lived alone, and whose custom it was to boil a huge pot of oatmeal at one time, and eat of it daily until it was finished. One evening the farmer came home to see that some oatmeal was still left in the pot, though many days had passed, and that there was a green fur covering it. He stared rebelliously at the mess. Finally, he reached for the remains of a bottle of firewater from the shelf above the table and said, "Now, friend, you sit down and eat up all that oatmeal and you shall have a nip of firewater."

Accordingly, he sat down and shoveled all the mess into his mouth, and swallowed it with a shudder. Then his eyes lit up as he fondled the bottle, stood up and replaced it on the shelf unopened.

"I trick myself," he said contentedly.

Yes, the tolerance, the honesty, and that sometimes superhuman fortitude tempered with wry humor are qualities that endear Iceland to me.

As to when I am leaving, I must repeat that I am married to a patriot, which eliminates somewhat any choice in the matter. My problem is less whether to stay, than whether my life in Iceland can be more fulfilling than it has been. I know that this is a good place to bring up young children, and a kind country for growing old. As to its advantages for other ages—I can hope!